A Legacy of Shadows

To the Ladies
of the Park City Library
with all best wishes
and in friendship,

[signature]
July '99.
Cedar City

*This
book was
donated to the
Park City Library
by*
RoseMary Kelley

A Legacy of
SHADOWS

SELECTED POEMS

David Lee

 COPPER CANYON PRESS

Special thanks to Kloefkorn and Lebada, road warriors, for encouragement; David Caligiuri, Laura Popenoe, and Valerie Brewster for careful reading and suggestions; Michael Wiegers for friendship, humor, and convincing me that I ought to do this book; and Sam Hamill, without whom none of this would have ever happened. Praise, all: salud, amor, dinero, y bastante tiempo para gustarlos.

Copper Canyon Press gratefully acknowledges Ed Cain for the use of his painting on the cover.

The publication of this book was supported by grants from the Lannan Foundation, the National Endowment for the Arts, and the Washington State Arts Commission. Additional support was received from Elliott Bay Book Company, Cynthia Hartwig, and the many members who joined the Friends of Copper Canyon Press campaign. Copper Canyon Press is in residence with Centrum at Fort Worden State Park.

LIBRARY OF CONGRESS CATALOGING-IN-PUBLICATION DATA

Lee, David, 1944–
A legacy of shadows: selected poems / David Lee.
   p. cm.
ISBN 1-55659-098-9 (alk. paper)
ISBN 1-55659-097-0 (pbk.: alk. paper)

1. Farm life – United States Poetry. 2. Swine Poetry. I. Title.
PS3562.E338 A6 1999

811'.54 – DC21   99-6401
                                                        CIP

9 8 7 6 5 4 3 2 FIRST EDITION

COPPER CANYON PRESS
Post Office Box 271
Port Townsend, Washington 98368
www.ccpress.org

For Jan, with love

The process of life, poetically speaking, is a passing between dream and reality, and the mark of any man I could ever trust or care for is that he would never presume to say which is which.

MODEAN GILL

Contents

The Porcine Legacy

Loading a Boar   5
Behold   6
Jubilate Agno, 1975   7
Salvage Grain   11
The Pig Hunt   13
The Tale of the Graveblaster   18
Racehogs   19
Plowing   21
For Jan, with Love   23
Kolob at Evening   26
Nighthunting with John   27
Fall   28
Jan's Birthday   29
A Day of Mourning, 24 November '75   31
Dusk   32

Driving and Drinking

North to Parowan Gap   35
East to Paragonah   47
Back to the Valley   60

The Porcine Canticles

Barbed Wire   75
The Hay Swather   79

Tuesday Morning, Loading Pigs   82
Tuesday Morning, Driving to the
    Auction in Salina   84
The Chain Letter (An American Tragedy)   86
The Muffler and the Law   95
Culture   104
The Real Estate   105
Mean   110
Friday Afternoon, Feeding Pigs   118
Building a Farrowing Pen   123
The Farm   127
Aftermath   128
Balaam   129
Epilogue   133

Day's Work

Morning   139
After an All-Night Farrow   140
Sonnet on the Sun, Rising   141
Phone Call   142
January: Unloading Feed   144
Fence Repair   145
Faith Tittle   150
Building Pigpens   156
Coyote Dope   162
The Tree   164
Feeding   177
Fat   185
Arthritis   188
Separating Pigs   196
Morning Coffeebreak   198
Machinery   199
Castrating Pigs   208
Edna Mae   221

Still Life:
    Lightning Above the North Fields   223
Hired Hand   224
Digging Postholes   226
The Feed Store Salesman   231
Bargains   233
Taking a Break   238
Shoveling Rolled Barley   240
August: Midnight Farrow   243
Hauling Hogs   244
September 1st   247
September   252
Roofing the Barn   253
Evening   262
Coda   263
Pain   266

My Town

Prelude   277
Terrace Mound   278
Ugly   280
Fruit Trees   286
Preacher   288
Deaf   293
Doc   295
Bryant Williamson   302
Clean   307
Fast   309
Potts Coal Mine, Inc.   312
Lazy   318
The Sawmill Road   322
No Lazy S Ranch   329
Interlude   338
Curley   341

Jesse   346
Vera   348
Broken Leg   352
The Wart   356
Idyll   371
Haystacking   372
Brothers   380
The Landrum Geese   382
Bobby Joe   392
Willie and the Water Pipe   393
Postlude   398
Benediction   401

Covenants

Psalm Written After Reading Cormac
    McCarthy and Taking a Three-
    Hour Climb to the Top of
    Pine Valley Mountain   407
Cigarettes   408
Whiskey   411
Neighbors   415
What Happened When Bobby Jack
    Cockrum Tried to Bring Home
    a Pit Bulldog, or What His Daddy
    Said to Him That Day   421
Rhapsody for the Good Night:
    Christmas Eve '94   422

About the Author   433

A Legacy of Shadows

The Porcine Legacy

Loading a Boar

We were loading a boar, a goddam mean big sonofabitch and he
jumped out of the pickup four times and tore out my stockracks and
rooted me in the stomach and I fell down and he bit John on the
knee and he thought it was broken and so did I and the boar stood
over in the far corner of the pen and watched us and John and I just
sat there tired and Jan laughed and brought us a beer and I said,
"John it aint worth it, nothing's going right and I'm feeling half dead
and haven't wrote a poem in ages and I'm ready to quit it all," and
John said, "shit, young feller, you aint got started yet and the reason's
cause you trying to do it outside yourself and aint looking in and if
you wanna by god write pomes you gotta write pomes about what
you know and not about the rest and you can write about pigs and
that boar and Jan and you and me and the rest and there aint no way
you're gonna quit," and we drank beer and smoked, all three of us,
and finally loaded that mean bastard and drove home and unloaded
him and he bit me again and I went in the house and got out my paper
and pencils and started writing and found out John he was right.

Behold

And came forth like Venus from an ocean of
heat waves, morning in his pockets and the buckets in his hands
he emerged from the gray shed, tobacco and wind
pursed together in song from his tight lips he gathered day
and went out to cast wheat before swine. And in
his mind he sang songs and thought thoughts, images of clay
and heat, wind and sweat, dreams of silver and
visions of green earth twisting the cups of his mind
he crossed his fence of wire, the south Utah steppes
bending the air into corners of sky he entered
the yard to feed his swine. And his pigs, they come.

Jubilate Agno, 1975

Christopher Smart, 1722–1771
Blackula Poland China, 1971–1975
(memorandus)

For I will consider my black sow Blackula.

For she is the servant of the god of the feed bucket and serveth him.

For she worships the god in him and the secret of his pail in her way.

For this is done by screams of incantation at the appointed hour and lusty bites of daily communion.

For she stands with forelegs upon the top rail of the wooden fence in supplication.

For she grunts her thanks while she eats.

For she stands for the red boar with closed eyes at the appointed hour.

For having done she lies in the mud to consider herself.

For this she performs in ten degrees.

For first she rolls in her wallow to cover her body.

For secondly she lies still to feel the wet.

For thirdly she stretches her length and casts her belly to the sun.

For fourthly she exhales God's air in huge sighs.

For fifthly she rises and examines her feed trough that replenishment might miraculously appear.

For sixthly she scratches her side against the fence.

For seventhly she scratches her jowl with delicate pastern swipe.

For eighthly she smells the breeze to ascertain the red boar's presence.

For ninthly she returns to her mud and plows large holes in the earth.

For tenthly she lies again in the wallow to cool her frame.

For having considered her world she will sleep and dream dreams of herself and her god and the red boar.

For like Eve for softness she and sweet attractive Grace was formed.

For the red boar lusteth mightily and foameth at the mouth for her.

For he might escape and enter her pen.

THE PORCINE LEGACY   7

For if he does this in a nonappointed hour she will scream loudly
and discourage his kisses.
For her belly is full and needeth no more.
For in one month she will bring forth life in abundance.
For in her last litter she farrowed eight piglets of the red boar.
For three were black and five were red.
For she raised them all and laid on none.
For one in eight is normally crushed by the sow.
For she is exceedingly good in all that she does.
For she is surely of the tribe of Elephant and forgetteth not.
For she weighs near six hundred pounds.
For she has ears of tremendous size.
For she is heavy.
For a large sow is a term of the Titan Elephant.
For she has the appetite of a bird and would eat the day long which
in debt her master suppresses.
For he would not have her too fat or his checkbook hollow.
For he keeps her well-fed and she breaks no fence.
For she grunts in pleasure from the mud when he scratches her ears.
For she is a tool of God to temper his mind.
For when she eats her corn she turns and shits in her trough.
For her master is provoked but hereby learns patience.
For she is an instrument for him to learn bankruptcy upon.
For he lost but four dollars each on the last litter of pigs.
For this is admirable in the world of the bank.
For every man is incomplete without one serious debt or loss.
For she provides this with her good faith.
For every farm is a skeleton without a mortgage.
For the Lord admonished black sows when he said lay up no stores
of treasure on earth.
For she prohibits this daily.
For she is a true child of God and creature of the universe.
For she is called Blackula which is a derivative of the Devil, but false.
For she does worship her God and Savior.

For she was given her name for breaking a fence and eating Jan's
    garden beets.
For when Jan came with a stick and wrath she lifted her head and smiled.
For her teeth and mouth were stained with red beet pulp.
For Jan dropped the stick and laughed.
For she looked like a six-hundred-pound vampire.
For she was called Blackula.
For we feed her red beets daily to watch her smile.
For she is humble when well-fed.
For she makes her point well when she is hungry.
For there is nothing swifter than a sow breaking fence when she desires.
For there is nothing more beautiful than a sow in full run when being
    chased through a garden.
For there is no sound more pure than her scream when she is hit with
    a stick.
For she is meek in all aspects when satisfied.
For when John Sims saw her lying in mud he proclaimed her majesty.
For he whistled and called her a pretty sonofabitch.
For he offered to trade his beat-up truck for her straight across.
For she has divine spirit and is manifest as a complete pig.
For she is tame and can be taught.
For she can run and walk and sleep and drink and eat.
For she can scream at the red boar.
For she allows her ears and belly to be scratched.
For she allows small children to ride her back.
For she sleeps in mounds of straw at night.
For she produces litters of healthy black and red pigs.
For she can root the earth.
For she can carry sticks in her mouth.
For she will grunt when she is addressed.
For she can jump not far but hard.
For dried earth cracks in the places where she walks.
For she is hated by the breeders of cattle and sheep.
For the former loses more money than I do on his stock.

For the latter fears her mind.

For she has no wool and will not blindly follow his steps.

For he carries no bucket of feed.

For she litters twice per year.

For he litters but once.

For her belly is firm and can take much abuse.

For from this proceeds her worth.

For I perceive God's mystery by stroking her teats.

For I felt tiny lumps of flesh within and knew they were alive.

For the life is the physical substance which God sends from Heaven to sustain the appetites of men.

For God has blessed her womb and the red boar's seed.

For they multiply in ecstasy at the appointed time.

For God has blessed her in many ways.

For God has given her the red beets to eat.

For God has given the water for her to drink.

For God has allowed the water to turn to mud in a place for her to lay.

For she cannot fly to the mountain streams, though she walks well upon the earth.

For she walks the earth heavy upon tiny feet.

For she treads all the rows of the summer garden.

For she can jump the fence.

For she can push it down.

For she can eat.

Salvage Grain

1

On the way to the feedstore
John sez we oughta be able to get the grain
for two dollars and so when the man bid
two and a quarter I sez that's that
and John moves behind Jan and whispers
bid two thirty and I sez what?
and he winks and I bid and the man bid
two and a half and John calls him a sonofabitch
to Jan and the other man looks at me
to see if I'll bid and I shake my head no
and John he punches me and sez three
and I sez what? and he sez three
and I sez three and the man calls me
a sonofabitch to his wife and the other man sez
what's your name and John sez tell him Homer
and I sez what? and John winks again and I sez
Homer Melvin because that's all I can think
and he tells the secretary to put down Homer
for ten tons and we go home.

2

A month later the man calls John
and sez where's Homer Melvin? and John sez
oh him? he died and the man sez but
he bought all this grain and what am I going to do
and John sez damn he's sorry he don't know
but he'd take it off his hands for two dollars
a hundred and the man sez no and hangs up
but calls John back in an hour and sez
come get it and John calls me

and I get Jan to write a check for two hundred
for our half and we go to meet John to go
to the feedstore and the man looks at me funny
and sez what's your name and I say Dave
and he sez isatso? and John sez you damn right
he's Dave what'd you think I made him
my partner for? and we load our two-dollar
grain in John's and my truck and go home.

The Pig Hunt

After reading an article in Peterson's Hunting,
January, 1975

1

What if you get caught without a season? Nothing.
Don't despair. Try a farmer. Try a chicken. Old hens,
young layers, some will even fly and can be taken on the wing.
Or a duck. They limp when they walk and this provides more sport
in an unsteady target. Or for the more serious, the mature,
the elite, the by-God-American-sportsMAN there's pigs.
I mean find a farmer, a real down-to-earth, grinning
illiterate, sweaty son-of-bitch dirt farmer who raises pigs,
preferably crossbred spotted variety (spots show up well in
photographs) (spotted pig hides make beautiful rugs) (spots
make wonderful targets). Pay him market price for a hog—
boars are the bargain, at least ten cents a pound below top-
market swine, and there is danger in tusks and balls and foam
and boars generally do not move swiftly and make nice stationary
prey for the hunter—and give him five for his trouble,
there's no license anyway so you're still ahead. Have him turn
the beast out of his pen into the field. A cornfield is nice,
good concealment, straight rows to sight down, he will browse
while you stalk. Or sagebrush is better. He can hide,
you can hide, the farmer can hide and watch, and your wife's brother
can hide and follow with the Kodak while you hunt the boar.
Use a bow. A rifle is too swift, too easy. A bow is right.
Stalk him quietly, creep close through the forage, wear
your camouflage suit, stay downwind and keep the sun in his eyes,
remember this animal is dangerous, never walk between him
and the feed trough or he may charge. Close in,
sight carefully, place the arrow behind his front leg
to catch the lungs and heart. Have a second ready,

he has strength and may run or attack or squeal if wounded.
Pull a full arrow length, feel the surge of power as you peer
down the length of your shaft, tighten your lips as the smooth death
prepares to take wing, release the string and listen
as the behemoth screams in anguish, shoot again as he attempts to rise
and escape, sing as the beast yields to your triumph,
the song of songs, *to eat, to live, to hunt, this is life,* glory
in the red foam spreading the earth, secure in your fame
for you have toed the mark once more and again are affirmed as Man.

2

I couldn't believe him
he sez I'll buy your hog
and I sez you don't raise hogs
and he sez I know
but I'll buy yours
and I sez sixty dollars
and he nods good and gives me
sixty-five and sez let him out
and that silly shitass chases him
down the field with a bow
and arrow until the hog stops
to eat some alfalfa
and he gets down on his belly
crawls close and shoots and
shoots and shoots and the hog
goes down he yells
and his brother-in-law comes up
takes his picture with the dead hog
arrows sticking out all over
and he keeps saying
by God I put him away didn't I?

3

The art is in the lens.
An idiot can aim and press
the button, the artist focuses the moment.
Eternity. The action of the chase
as they run through tangled sage,
the saga of life and death
stalking each other
a glimpse of sunlight filling
old paths as they meet
captured forever in the exposed film:
man and boar and artist.

4

Pig, I hunted you in the old ways
stalked you as I did once
long ago before the concrete and asphalt
before they put you in small pens
to breed away your spirit and soul.

Pig, in death I gave you life
the moment of truth when we stood
face-to-face again as it was
and should be, when you saw your death
and knew and stood in majesty, unafraid.

Pig, now we share the eternal bond
of brotherhood, your blood mingled
in mine throbbing the years
until we rise to meet again in perfection
and know forever the ecstasy of the hunt.

Pig, sleep well. Gather your dreams
for the day when we become one.

5

I don't mind the picture on the wall,
men gather trophies to spell their lives
as corners gather dust and memory.

I don't mind Jim's signature in the corner
or the sign Don made, "Note the short
but sharp tusks beneath the monster's lip."

I don't mind hearing the endless tales
of brotherhood and freedom and communion
every night in the dining room.

What I do mind is the bristles spreading
across the floor, plugging my vacuum
each time he walks across his rug.

What I do mind is the kids
bringing in their friends from school
to see the big pig Daddy shot.

What I do mind is the questions
I'm asked by my friends, the sly smiles,
the time I heard Joan call me Mrs. Hogslayer.

That I mind a lot.

6

We were building fence
and it was hot. John strung
and stretched and I followed, hammering
steeples. He worked and I worked
and we both sweat a lot.
John, I said finally when I got tired,

I read in this magazine about farmers
renting out their hogs to hunters.
John didn't say anything so I went on,
they let hunters come in and hunt
their hogs. I mean, I said, the hunters
come in and pay them market price
and a little for their trouble
to hunt their pigs in their fields
with a bow and arrow.

John didn't turn but went on working
so I worked some more
until I caught up to him
ready to say reckon you ought to do that
because John would say something
and I'd laugh because it would
be funny. John puts down the roll of fence
before I talk and sits on it
then John says, I seen that book
that ignorant goddam book
and I'd like to find the man
who shot that pig and the farmer
and the bow and arrow
the whole goddam mess and lock them
in a room with the dead hog
and let them stay there forever
that's what I'd do.
What kind of a goddam man would even think
of something like that?
And he started working again
and I worked
and we built the fence
and I was glad I hadn't said anything
about hunting John's pigs.

The Tale of the Graveblaster

On the way to the auction in Salina to sell our pigs John told a story about a graveblaster he knew in Pioche. Not a digger, the ground was too hard so he had to blast his graves out with dynamite. John couldn't remember the man's name but he had a son named Manuel who the story was about anyway. There was a day when the father was ill and had to be taken to the hospital in Ely. Afternoon, the mortician called and asked for the father; only Manuel was left to blast the grave. He loaded his father's truck with the sticks from the case, fused the charge, walked behind a small knoll and detonated the explosives. The blast carved a huge gap in the earth which spread much farther than Manuel had anticipated. Nearby graves were upthrust and several coffins disinterred and scattered profusely about the area. John's story struck me as being somewhat sardonically humorous and I laughed. Incredulous, John slowed his truck, cut me off with a glance. "It aint funny you sonofabitch," he said. "That was his daddy's grave he was blasting."

Racehogs

John calls and sez Dave
when I say hello and I say hello John
and he sez come down Dave
you gotta see what I got
I say fine I'll be right there and he sez
bring Jan I'll show her too
and I said I will
so Jan and I got in the car to see
what John bought.

John bought four hogs
starved half to death, bones out
everywhere, snouts sharp enough
to root pine trees and the longest damn legs
I've seen. What do you think? he sez
and I don't say anything so he sez
I sez what do you think? and I say
them's pretty good looking racehogs John
and he sez what? and I tell him
I heard about a place in Japan or California
(because he's never been there) where they
have a track and race hogs
on Tuesday nights and he sez do they
pay much? and I say yes or so I heard
maybe a hundred to win and he sez
goddam and I say those hogs
ought to be good with them long legs
and skinny bodies and he sez goddam.
Jan's walked off so I go find her
but she's mad and says I ought not to do that
and I say oh I was just bullshitting
but when we come back John's standing

by the fence throwing little pieces of feed
all around the pen making the hogs
hurry from one place to the next
and when I get up close he's smiling
and I can hear him whisper
while he throws the feed
run you skinny fuckers, run.

Plowing

1

All my life, broken ground.
Shovels. John Deere bangers. Sticks, cats, hoes.
Always forgotten people speak
old ways, lost ways, fossils.

I found an old plow,
bought leather straps, borrowed John's
half-blind Dan   *n goddammit boy*
don let that sonnybitch kick ya he's mean bastard
sed John, helped me with harness.

2

My anticipations all misplaced,
early plowed under. Expected sun
and flesh, tracings and neck leaders,
mind drifting to Kolob's breezes,
tired arms, hoarse throat.

Found wind, thick clods. John's Dan
walked easy, followed his good eye
in straight lines. I moved, something habitual,
behind, stepping over turned earth,
shy at harness,
precariously balanced on one of the world's edges,
wind against my hair
exploding into afternoon   *god aint he sumin*
that mule's so old he carried Moses inta Jewsalem
and he aint forgot a goddam thang
wind and earth and animal
the only geometry.

3

All my life I've heard death
takes us to the cycle's center,
where we should be. Crystals,
clusters. We exist within, know
both sides at once. Perfect definition.

And that life is broken parabola.
We wander against wind, random circles,
no closer to center, glimpses,
shadows and edges   *I caint tell ya how to do it boy*
it's gonna be there in ya bones or it aint shit for nowhere
the world inside. And I followed John's mule,
my boots relaxed in stillness, shattered dust,

plowed earth, wind, sky.
And John walked beside, talked of hog markets,
hollow bones, lakebottoms and forgotten ways.
The moon swallowed dusk. Our image
crystallized against a backdrop of night.

For Jan, with Love

1

John he comes to my house
pulls his beat-up truck in my drive
and honks
Dave John sez Dave my red sow
she got pigs stuck and my big hands they won't go
and I gotta get them pigs out
or that fucker she's gonna die
and I sez John goddam
we'll be right down and John sez Jan
he yells JAN where's Jan she's got little hands
she can get in there and pull them pigs
and I sez Jan and he sez Jan and Jan comes
what? Jan sez and John sez tell Jan Dave
and I sez Jan John's red sow's got pigs
stuck and his hand's too big and won't go
and he's gotta get them pigs out
or that fucker's gonna die (John he turns
his head and lights a cigarette)
(he don't say fuck to no woman)
and Jan she sez well let's go
and we get in John's beat-up damn truck
and go to pull John's pigs

2

John's red sow she doesn't weigh
a hundred and sixty pounds
but he bred her to his biggest boar
and had to put haybales by her sides
so the boar wouldn't break
her back because Carl bet five dollars

he couldn't and John he bet
five she could and John he won
but Carl enjoyed watching anyway

3

John's red sow was laying
on her side hurting bad
and we could see she had a pig
right there but it wouldn't come she
was too small and John sez see
and I sez I see that pig's gotta come out
or that fucker's gonna die
and Jan puts vaseline on her hands
and sez hold her legs and I hold her legs
and Jan goes in after the pig
and John gets out of the pen and goes
somewheres else

Jan she pulls like hell pretty soon
the pig come big damn big little pig
dead and I give Jan more vaseline and she goes
back in to see about any more
and John's red sow pushes hard on Jan's arm
up to her elbow inside and Jan sez
there's more help me and I help
another pig damn big damn dead comes
and John's red sow she seems better
and we hope that's all

4

John's red sow won't go
out of labor so we stay all night
and John brings coffee and smokes
and flashlight batteries and finally Jan

can feel another pig but John's red sow's
swole up tight and she can't grab hold
but only touch so I push her side
and she grunts and screams and shits all over Jan's arm
and Jan sez I got it help me and I help
and we pull for a goddam hour and pull
the pig's head off

and I sez oh my god we gotta get that pig now
or that fucker's gonna die for sure
and John sez what happened? and Jan
gives him a baby pig's head in his hand
and John goes somewheres else again
while Jan goes back fast inside
grabbing hard and John's red sow
hurts bad and Jan sez I got something help me
and I help and we start taking that pig out
piece by piece

5

Goddam you bitch don't you die
Jan yells when John's red sow don't help no more
and we work and the sun comes up
and finally we get the last piece of pig out
and give John's red sow a big shot of penicillin
her ass swole up like a football
but she don't labor and John sez
is that all? and Jan wipes her bloody arms
on a rag and sez yes and John climbs in
the pen and sez how's my red sow?
and we look and go home and go to bed
because John's red sow that fucker she died

Kolob at Evening

I went to the edge of the wood
in the color of evening...

JOHN HAINES

The color of evening washed at my feet
and I dreamed years of dying suns
buried in the west end of Kolob Lake

old fishermen on their gray rocks
beaver and swallows mating in the eclipse
of twilight and dusk
sink in the splashing reflection
to the meadows beneath the mirror
where fat trout graze like hogs
on September alfalfa

a subterranean world of sunken campfires
where I sit before black ashes
and drink lakewater from a rusted cup
while the sun falls and drives the fish
upward to explode into night

silver gods leaping to swallow the moon.

Nighthunting with John

Last night I went hunting
hogfeed with John
up and down the black alleys
splitting a case of Lucky
looking for the good spots
unburned barrels where expensive folks
pile their scraps for John's sows –
the same as you'n me eat onliest more often
he sez a dozen times
between stops before he sez shit
and turns off his lights
and slips his beat-up truck quiet
down the backside of West 5th
where he used to live.

Gotta watch them damn sorry folks
he sez they leave the best stuff
and then wait in the dark so you don't get it
and you better get down in the seat
and he stops and I get down and drink beer
and listen while he sorts through their trash quiet
putting the edibles in the truck bed
along with anything else that looks good
and he gets in and slams the door
and honks and drives off fast
and scrapes the barrels with his beat-up truck
and all the lights in the house come on
and he laughs and drinks beer
and sez that's enough let's go
last time I come and banged the cans
those bastards tried to shoot holes in my tires.

Fall

This day when I see the white moon
through a dry branch of another fall at my window,
my fingers stretch to the fire by Kolob
raking and sifting the lifeless ash body.
I rise toward the door drawing crisp wind and
yellow grass in large draughts.

This day I leave her body,
stiff with sleep, in the warm house
to climb toward pale aspen canyons
behind my house. Gasping for breath
I see old initials my father left,
hold my face against cool white bark.

And I return to my ten acres
with its pigs, ripe corn, Jan, still asleep,
aspen powder on my collar, chokecherry-etched
breath, blood streaked in the lines of my hands.

Jan's Birthday

I saved seventy dollars to buy Jan a present
this time because I forgot last year
and went to town to see what I could find.
I found John and he bought a round
and I bought a round and John sez
let's go watch the auction and we drank another beer
and got in my truck and bought a sixpack
and went. They ran a pureblood
Spotted Poland China sow in and John sez
that's a good one and the man sez who'll start this
at thirty and I felt good about remembering
Jan's birthday and said I will and he started
auctioning but nobody bid and John sez
hope she makes you a nice hog Dave
and I told the man upstairs about Jan's
birthday while he made out the ticket
but he didn't hear and John sez give her to Jan
and she cost sixty-four dollars and ninety-six cents
and after the beer I had thirty-eight cents left
when we loaded up that spotted sow.

I was mad and John sez give her to Jan Dave again
and he bought another beer and I drove
my truck to Woolworth's and went in with my beer
in my hand and bought thirty-eight cents'
worth of red ribbon and the lady tied a bow
and gave me a piece of paper so I wrote
For Jan, With Love and John held the spotted sow
by the leg and I tied the ribbon with the bow
around her neck while the lady watched
and said oh my god over and over
the sow screaming like hell stopping cars

and the sheriff drove up and said we had to move
because we were impeding traffic so I pinned the note
to the ribbon and said you gonna help me?
and John sez no I got work to do but you
been to college you'll think of something
so I drove John to his truck
stole two of his beers got drunk
and hit a Piute Indian who hit me back
and a man called the sheriff who sez goddam Dave
and he sez I gotta get out of town or he'll arrest me
and I say Ira I can't drive I'm drunk and Jan will kill me
because it's her birthday and Ira said goddam Dave again
made me sit in the back with the hog
and a deputy named Melvin drove his car to my house
behind us with the red light flashing
while Ira drove me and Jan's seventy-dollar
happy-birthday present home.

A Day of Mourning, 24 November '75

I had to sell my black sow Blackula today.
She has become fallow, rejects the boar,
has no pigs and eats too much to keep.
Alas, goddammit. I loved that pig.

Dusk

In the snow yesterday's tracks deepen.
A flock of starlings crosses my window and breaks
the monotony of the sky. A last leaf falls,
crosses the yard in front of me, scuttles
over the crust toward the sow's pen,
makes small tattered prints. Nothing better to do,
I pull on my heavy jacket and cap and go to chase it down,
a gift for Jan. The red sow pauses and lifts her head
from the trough as I pass.

Oblivious of where I am, I wade the snow to the fence.
Wind fills my eyes with frozen leaves, an etched forest
in my blurred vision of night.

A gust bounces against my body. Steps away I see the leaf
on a smooth patch of snow. I pick it up,
then toss it into the north currents. It drifts
beyond my fence like a small animal, fleeing,
worlds twisting away behind like breath. I look away,
to the west, find night already there.

Driving and Drinking

North to Parowan Gap

Turn right up there
and get off these pavements
there aint no sense
to holding up the traffic
and we aint hurrying
you just turn there and that dirt road
goes out to the Gap
where them Indins wrote on them rocks

I remember the first time
I ever got drunk. Me and my brother
we was following this branch back home in Misippi
when we seen a trail leading off
and he knew but I didn't
he's older'n I was and been down them trails
so's we went down and found it
any time you find a trail off a branch
you follow it it'll take you to a
still that's how them revenuers find them
or maybe somebody's shithouse
but that'll be by their house close
so you know so's anyway
we found it and they had all this beer
that's the first boilings out of the mash
before they make the whiskey
and my brother he broke off these cane stems
to make straws and we got to sipping
that beer by god I passed out
I hadn't had that befores and he got scairt
and had a hell of a time getting me home
where he told Mama he didn't know what happened

maybe I fell or got snake bit or cow kicked
cause she'd of beat him into next week
if he sed I was drunk cause I was too little
Mama about had a worm of course
I don't remember I was passed out
and thot I wouldn't live cause her brother
got kicked in the head and woke up a idiot and
stayed that way naturally
he got kicked by a horse
you can still see the print of that horseshoe
on the back of his head
he don't look a day older'n the day it happened
so she went for the doctor
that was quite a trip we lived
12 mile outside town and didn't have no car
she walked the whole way but the doctor he give her
a ride back that doctor he come
looked at me and he sez he'll be okay
soon as he sobers up and they say Mama cried
and raised all kind of hell
the next day was my birthday and I was 9
I guess that's why I member
she was so mad she made me a cake
after I eat a piece she thowed
the rest away and wouldn't let nobody else have none

so's this other time we found this branch
and went down there was the biggest still
I ever seen they was making barrels of whiskey
by the wagonload and I don't know how
they did it that still wasn't a mile from our house
we never seen no smoke nor smelled it
we figgered maybe they's shining at night
it must of been white folks or rich niggers

(that's what we called them back then) cause
they had money so me and my brother
we went home and hitched the wagon to come back
we stoled 2400 pound of sugar
in daylight, Lord Jesus that was stupid
we could of been shot but I guess nobody seen us
I heard God takes care of kids and idiots
that's where my brother he got his finger cut off
we was hurrying and he must of got
his finger in the leaf springs and I thowed
this sugar up and he sez ouch and that's all
till we's almost home and he sez look here
I done cut my finger off and it was gone for sure
Mama got scairt but we hid it and
give most of it away or fed it to the hogs
we didn't have no money so that was a good find
me and my brother we went back the next day
when Mama wasn't looking cause she sed
to keep our butts out of there or we'd wake up dead
them shiners they don't want no companies
but they wasn't nothing there
they'd moved that whole still that night
so's you couldn't tell it'd ever been there
we looked around but didn't find
his finger it was gone too and
we never heard a sount

Mama she made wine at home
outa berries and grapes and stuff and we'd hep
she'd make little jars for us
but wouldn't put in no sugar so it wouldn't
make no alcohol just grape juice
when she'd get to working we'd get that sugar and
slip it in the jars and close them up while she didn't know

she thot it was fine we was drinking juice good
for vitamins in the wintertime
we thot it was fine too

Mama just whupped me bad one time
because I was the youngest
it wasn't my fault I didn't mean no harm
I found this bull snake and put him in the corncrib
to eat up the mice that was eating the corn
leaving rat shit all over to stink
them rat turds make a building smell up
worse then skunk piss cause it don't go away
stinks like sorry folks live there
so I thot it'd be a good idear
but I forgot about it until Mama
she went out to get some corn and grabbed holt of
that snake because she couldn't see good
in the dark and I was standing there in the door
heard her yell by god she come out of that crib fast
and couldn't let go of that snake
she choked it to death and beat me with it
all the way back to the house
I'd of rather she'd of used a switch
by then I was scared of that snake too
it hurt like hell I won't pick up no snake
now for nobody. But it did eat up
a whole buncha mice so it wasn't a real bad
idear like some I've saw

this other time we
lost our milkcow and had to go find her
we let her run loose but this time she didn't come back
so we went to look and we found this still
these niggers was running. It was niggers we knew

so we started talking but they wouldn't give us
no whiskey because they knew Mama would kill them
if she found out and she always did
we just talked for awhile about whiskey and wormen and
Jesus things niggers talk about and after a time
here comes Mama and we thot we'd bought the farm
cause we posta be looking for that cow
and had forgot about that
Mama she didn't say nothing but just walked up
stood there awhile and then she sez
what you niggers got buriet over there?
and we seen this grave we hadn't noticed before
but we could tell it was a grave
aint it funny how you caint never get a grave
hid to where it don't show?
them nigger men went to stirring
one sed oh no Miz Sims that aint no grave
she sed don't you lie to me Leonas Johnston
that's a grave and you done kilt my milkcow
and buriet it there Leonas he sez
no Ma'am we aint done kilt yo milkcow
that aint what's buried theah she sez to me
and my brother to go home and get the shovel
so we'll just see cause it was a fresh grave
them niggers all come over then they sez
now Miz Sims we aint seen yo milkcow
she sez for them to all go strait to hell they done
kilt it and buried it them niggers got to dickering
they give Mama a hundred dollars for our cow
so we wouldn't dig it up the cow wasn't
worth that but she took the money and we went home
2 days later that cow come back with a new calf
we didn't know she was gonna have Mama
sez now aint that something? I lived there

12 more years and I never did go back to see what
was in that grave I really didn't much
want to find out I guess

that damn cow got us in all sorts of troubles
she's always running off and we couldn't find her but
we never done too awful much shining ourselves
just wine and a little whiskey for us now and then
Mama she never liked it much
but this one time it got rough we didn't have
no money at all and the crops didn't come in
sides the revenuers had put the hammer down
and the reglar shiners cut off
so me and my brother we thot wot the hell
we needed money and besides if they caught us
they had to feed us in jail baloney and grits and gravy
we set up this little still not much
but we made this deal for 30 gallons in pint jars
and that'd help a little to get thu winter
we cooked her up and it was a good batch we
made us some too and got it all put up in the cellar
on Saturday night these niggers was gonna come get it
but me and my brother we got this other job killing hogs
so we had to go that day but sed we'd be back fore night
well that morning here comes this law
he knocks on the door but Mama seen him coming
she hid and wouldn't open the door he yelled
and knocked for a long time and looked all over
in the yard and shithouse and barn but he never
opened the cellar and then left
Mama she's scairt she carried all that whiskey
out to the barn and poured it out on the ground
and warshed the jars and then busted up the still and
buried it so by the time we got back it was done

and that evening here come the law again
he knocks on the door and Mama sez what you want?
and he sez Miz Sims you know whar your cow is?
she sez my cow? he sez yas
she sez what cow? and he sez you only got one cow
she sez oh that one? he sez yas and it's breechy
and done broke down 3 fences and knocked down
a shithouse and kicked a dog and mebbe broke its head
open but she found her a bull by god and she's bred
and you gotta come get her right now
she sez oh that one and he sez yas so my brother
he went with him to get her and then Mama
she started bawling she sez oh John I thot he's after
the whiskey and I sez no just the cow the whiskey's okay
she sez oh no it aint and I sez what?
so she took me to the barn to show me where she
poured it out by god there was 3 sows and all their pigs
laying there deader'n hell I sez what the shit?
Mama sez oh my god I done kilt our hogs
I sez I sez what the hell's going on? she sez
the law's here before and I thot he's after the shine
so I poured it all out and it kilt our hogs
and she commenced to bawling real bad and I felt sorry
but when I looked again them hogs wasn't dead
but they's so drunk they couldn't get up
and could only barely breathe
it was 4 days before we could get them out
of that barn and then they'd break back in
ever chance they'd find and it was all that cow's fault
but them niggers never did even come to buy it anyway
I never did find out why not
but we didn't make no more whiskey to sell
Mama sez she couldn't take that no more

I always had the bad luck
finding dead bodies
some people have the touch for it
some just don't. The first one
besides what might of been in them niggers' grave
was this feller that they thot was lost
and put him on the radio for everbody
to look for so we all went out to hep
I found him but he wasn't lost
but dead in his car by this dirt tank
where he'd drove to shoot hisself
he couldn't shoot straight for shit
he'd meant to put the pistol in his mouth
and blow his brains out the back but he missed and
shot his face off but he was dead anyway
I always wondered if it hurt or not
the dumb sonofabitch
they couldn't even open his box at the funeral
so's we could see most people
just had to take my word for it

and then this feller got drownt in the river
we had to get him out because the fish
would eat him then you couldn't sell no fish
to the niggers for a month they'd think
they's eating people or something
we'd get out the boats and the hooks
and drag the mud
sometimes you'd find him sometimes not
we'd always spread the word we'd
got him out and they wasn't no fishbites
this time we couldn't raise this one so
we all anchored up the river
and they blowed up dynamites in the water

to make him float up
I don't know why that works but it does
I had this nigger friend in my boat
he was drinking whiskey and they
blowed some up by us blubblubblub
here he come up right beside us
by god it like to of scairt me to death
he floated right over to my boat
so I hooked him when I looked at that nigger
he was all white like me he was ascairt so
I sez do you reckon we oughta pull him
in the boat with us? he sez whar?
and I sez in here and he sez whar
in this boat? and I sez yas and he sez Mista John
if you let him in this heah boat I's getting out
right now I sez Heavy you caint swim
and he sez whar? so I sez heah
just like the way niggers talk
he sez Mista John if they's to let some nasty dead man
in the boat with Jesus he just gets out and walks
on the watah what's good for Jesus is good fo
Heavy that's whar I sez to myself that's good for me too
I don't like touching no dead body neither
and won't do it that's what they pay them
people who go to college to learn how to do it for
but I acted like I was going to pull him in
Heavy he damn near turned that boat over
he was getting out I mean right now
by the time they come got him from us
and we got back to shore Heavy he was so drunk
he couldn't walk to his car I heard he
went and got babtized again next Sunday
he's so scairt

this other time I was running my trotline at night
I didn't have no license
and I was pulling my line in when it stuck
so I thought it was snagt or I had me a big catfish
on so's I took a wrap on my hand and
pulled hard it moved a little not much
so I wrapped it rount my back
like you hold a big hog with a nose loop
give a jerk and felt it give so's I pull
hard and hold my lantern out there's
somebody's arm sticking up out of the water
broke off his body at the shoulder
right in front of me oh my lord
it ascairt me terrible I peed right in my boot
I got out of there
finding bodies in the daytime's one thing
I aint staying around them at night
I called the sheriff and told him
he went and got it I heard
it was some feller who'd got wrapped up
in a chain and he fell in the river
I don't know how he done that
they was a reward and he kept it the sonofabitch
I couldn't do nothing
I didn't have no license
to run that trotline
by god sometimes I just hate the laws

I run a fish boat for years
on the river it was a good way to make
a little money back then
during the Depression it got so bad
to where one time the auction only offered us
a dollar apiece for top hogs then charged

20 cents to handle so's we had to take
over a hundred head out and shoot them
cause it wasn't worth it but I could
make enough to get by poaching fish
and selling them to the niggers
turtles too I never knew what they did
with them turtles but for awhile I'd go out
with a dip net I get a warshtub full
of baby turtles so's this man he'd come
give me a dollar a hundred
but the law come and made me quit
else he'd make it hot so's I couldn't sell fish
no more I've always wondered if he was
selling turtles too
I'd buy 5 gallons of whiskey and then fill
these half-pint jars half full then put water
soaked in tobacco in the rest and take
the whiskey and the fish to town
I'd pull up and honk here'd come
these niggers I'd sell them a half pint of whiskey
and a fish for a dollar but not just whiskey
I aint never been a bootlegger
they had to buy a fish or they couldn't have no whiskey
I'd wrap up the fish in newspaper
which was good cept I'd draw a crowd
round my car I'd have to keep moving round town
so's the law wouldn't start wondering
and come see they didn't much like selling whiskey
to niggers fish was all right
but fish never drew no crowd
them niggers would give me the nastiest damn dollar bills
I ever saw here'd come a big old fat womern
she'd reach down between her boosums
and pull out this piece of paper that you couldn't

even tell was money it was so greasy
I was almost ashamed to spend it
but not quite so I'd sell for awhile
then drive down a ways and honk and
sell some more one time I drove 5 miles
to the next town and was selling and here come
this nigger who'd walked the 5 miles to buy more whiskey
he still had his fish wrapped up in newspaper
under his arm Christ almitey I sold a lots of fish
that way. But then one day I got caught
the law thowed me in jail so I left Misippi
fore my trial I aint lived there since
that sheriff he's still the law and that's been 25 years ago
so's I just go back to visit sometimes

Pull off up there at the Gap will you
this here beer's hanging between my kidneys
and knees I better let some out.
We'll get on another road up there
we got plenty of time we can
put the lights on the rocks and
look at them Indin pitchers for a minute
we aint in no hurry are we?

East to Paragonah

We can go down this road now
it'll take us to Paragonah
but then you know that being as you
live there it's still a good place
and we got plenty of time.
I mean when I was a kid
we had to make our fun
there wasn't no moviehouses nor
money to raise hogs
and if you did have it they sold
for a dollar less than
nothing. We had to get by
with what we could find.
After I left Misippi
I and this friend was building shithouses
during the Depression and
we stayed in the upstairs of this gas station
in Kansas where we'd already built
these crappers out back
so when it got bored in the evenings
we went out to the wormen's
and drilt a hole beneath the seat and
built in a whupper made like a ping-pong paddle
on a wire so when we pulled
it'd flap up and whop whop whoever was
sitting on the throne on the ass
but she couldn't see who was whupping

the first was this lady tourist
in a out-of-state car without a husband
who didn't buy no gas but
just ran out back and we didn't know

if it'd work right so we waited
till we knew she'd be all hunkered good
and pulled hard twice and heard it
whop whop on her fat butt
Great Christ Jesus Almitey she yells
and comes running out of that shitter
her drawers down around her ankles
they didn't have no lasticks
back then the govament kept all the rubbers
to hisself but her drawers was stretched
out a yard at the top around her feet
when she run back to her car
we thot that was pretty funny
but she didn't buy no gas

about the same time
we had what we called the Great Shit Race
this guy Henry who was my friend
was real big he must of weight 250 or so
when somebody new would stop in town
who was little Henry'd start going on
about how he could beat me in a footrace
carrying a man and me not and
he'd bet money on it and pretty soon
this little guy would hear the money
and he'd sidle Henry and offer to be
carried for halves and Henry'd okay
and we go to race
outside town Henry'd lay down
on the ground on his face and he'd have
the little guy lay on him upside
down and tie him to Henry's back tight
with a rope cause Henry sez
it's easier to run that way

and when he stood up the guy's feet's
sticking up in the air because he's tied on
upside down and we line up and say go
and Henry runs a little ways and then sez oh
OH I gotta go to the bathroom and drops
his pants and squats
and that little guy's looking at him square
eyeball to asshole and he starts yelling oh no
please don't shit on ME and we all
have a laugh
we done this a few times till oncet
this guy was tied on Henry and when he
squats down that little fucker sez
you big sonofabitch you shit on me
I'll bite your nuts off real loud
and that scared Henry
he wouldn't Great Shit Race no more

there was this other lady
she came to the station in a big black car
and had a nigger driver who waited
and watched while the car got filt
while she went to pee so we snuck around
behind and pulled on the wire so
her ass'd get slapped and she by god
broke the door off she came out of there
so fast never yelled or nothing
but she was still holding her dress up
around her waist so's she wouldn't pee on it
and couldn't stop she was running
as fast as she could pissing 10 feet
ahead of her I never knew a womern
could piss that far and got in her car
and the nigger drove right off and never

paid for the gas but Mel (who owned the
station) didn't mind because she
left her purse in the shithouse and
it had 50 dollars she never did
come back for

I made these fart machines
out of a piece of clothes hanger and rubber bands
and a warsher (this was after the Depression
when I was more growed up) that I had
some fun with I'd go to the bar and put it
under me all wound up on the stool and then
at the right time I'd lean off and let it rip
on the plastic sounding like a big
butter-bean fart and we'd get a laugh
one time I and LaVerne went
to this bar in Boise and I told the bartender
and he sez yas go ahead and in comes
this Basque sheepherder that didn't have
3 fingers on one hand just a thumb and one other
to drink a beer and he sits down by me
the rest of the bar all but empty
but he's gotta sit right there so's I don't say
nothing for awhile and then lean over
and let that warsher unwound
that Basque he don't say nothing he looks
at me and shakes his head and
I say I'm sorry I had these ham and beans
for breakfast my stomach's clabbered and he
pats me on the shoulder and nods and tells
the bartender to make me a alkaseltzer
in my beer that'll feel better so while
he's not watching I wound the fart machine
up again tight and let it go again

real good
that Basque he grins and waves his hand
without no fingers and he sez
now is betta you don need no medichin
and LaVerne whispers and sez you better stop now
but I wound it up again and then let it off
that Basque he looks at me hard
then he stands up and walks out to
the middle of the floor and he skips and lifts
his leg up high and he lets
the biggest fart I've ever heard and sez
HOW WAS DAT VUN?
and LaVerne sez that's it I'm leaving
but before I can pick up my change he's
sitting back down and that fart
come with him all green
it was that kind that hangs on things
till it slides off and then lays on the floor
gasping and you know it's there and try not
to step on it because you can't get it
off your shoes and I sez
I didn't fart it was this machine
and he sez matchine?
and I sez yas and show it to him
and he sez vat do you guys
tink of nex time, huh?

the other one I member
was this old lady she came in a whole
carload and was crippled up to where
she had to walk with a cane
and I tell Henry we caint slap her ass
it'll break but he goes on down there
he was a crazy nigger

by god she must've been 80
or more it took her a half hour
to get to the shithouse and she's in good
and we hear whop and wait to hear whop
again but before it can come
here she is out of that crapper
running like a racehorse
all her arthritices gone and her drawers
dangling on one foot all the way
back to the car and she gets in
and slams the door and the rest of them
we can hear asking her what happened
but she didn't say nothing
so's after they left I went down
to the shithouse and her walking cane
was still there and I've got it somewheres
if I need it and by god she
pissed all over that shithouse door
I guess I built shithouses for 3 or 4 years
all over that damn Kansas

well after that I got this job
as a lectrician with the lectric company
I went round stringing wire and
fixing wire that's how I first came here
I built wires through these mountains and sed then
I'd like to come back and figgered mebbe I would
aint it funny? I was a lectrician 2 years
and I caint make that damn pump
down in my well work goddam near busted my ass
getting down in that hole yesterday
and got spider bit and wet to my ass
it still don't pump I shouldn't never crawl down in holes

oncet we was in Texas and there was this cave
with a long ditch running to it
that ditch sloped down to about 10 foot deep
with the cave at the bottom
I just had to go see what was in that hole
so's I walked down and went in and that's all
I member they was a deer in there
I didn't even know they was deers in Texas
that big sonofabitch come out of there
like a mayor out of a whorehouse
hit me right in the chest with his horns and
carried me out of that ditch and slung me off
at the top colder'n hell I don't even remember
being hit and it broke two ribs
they sed it was the biggest deer they'd ever saw
and I didn't even get to see it hurt so bad

then another time we was in Lousiana
we found this hole and I wanted to go in
so'd this nigger so I sez you go first and I'll foller
we crawled in all narrow as a chimley pipe
we could just barely get in then it opened up
in a room to where Wilber could stand up and he struck
a match and screams MAMA there's grunts
and we in a room full of them little javelina hogs
they's all scairt and trying to get out by god
somehow I got turned around in that tunnel
I still don't know how and come out
something else I don't know was how Wilber beat me outa
that hole but he did and still had the match in his hand
but it didn't stay lit I had hog tracks
all up my back them little fuckers just stomped
the piss outa both of us I never saw so many

in my whole life and don't want to again
I just don't know why God made holes in the ground for

one time I had to drive a long ways
to get to this other job I'd drove all day and half the night
I's tired and knew I couldn't drive no more
when I come to this one town I didn't know where I was
but there was this hotel so I stopped and went in
and rung the bell finally this man he come out I sez
I gotta have a room I'm sorry it's so late but I can't go
no more he sez well damn I'm sorry but we all full
I sez no shit? man I gotta find a bed somewheres
it's too cold to sleep in my car outside
it was winter and all
when he sez well there is this one room that has this
young feller in it he's a farm worker he sez
and come in for the weekend and there's 2 beds and
he sez if anybody needed the other one it was okay by him
so I sez that's okay by me how much?
he sez 4 dollars and that was fine so I paid him
and went up he was all asleep when I went in
so I didn't wake him up but just went to bed
a hour later I woke up but didn't roll over
just opened my eyes and he's standing there
without no clothes on but I could see he had
this big hard-on sticking out all over
I looked around the room and couldn't see
no jar of salve or hand lotion or bar of soap or nothing
so I sez to myself by god he aint screwing me
he was just standing there still not moving
I laid quiet for a long time but I couldn't take it
I's afraid he'd holler and jump on me
or with that hard-on just come and squirt
all over me and I wasn't gonna have that

so I finally set up and sez all right
you just go lay down on your bed right now
he jumped like he never knew I was even awake
and I'd scairt him but he backed up and
laid down I sez pull them covers up over you
and he did so I got out of bed and sez
you move just one time and I'll knock your goddam
head off you hear? you don't move a bit
and he didn't he never even sed a word
I put my clothes on and went down and
rung that bell that feller he come out and I sez
I don't mean to be polite but you got queers
in that room and I aint sleeping with no queer tonight
I'm too tired and they aint even no vaseline
he sez oh my god I'm sorry I didn't know that
I sez that's okay I aint tired no more
so he give me my 4 dollars back and I drove
the rest of the night and got to the job
and worked all that day I's too nervous
but I've always wondered what I'd of done
if he'd stood there and squirted stuff on my bed
where he thot I's sleeping

we went to the deep South
that's where my stomach went bad
eating that soft hominies and drinking
scum water when we couldn't find fresh
I wouldn't feed no hominies to a hog I hate them
so bad I eat so many then
but we had a funny thing happen
it wasn't funny to them that got caught though
I's glad as hell it wasn't me
we was near this one town stringing this wire
and here was this nigger mayor or something

we'd find whole towns of nigger people
that wasn't on the map
we figgered mebbe they's slaves that scaped
fore the war and still didn't know better
wasn't no white people living there
he was fat and wore a black hat
and had a umbrella he walked under
like them Englishmens do
and had a big house in the middle of town and
a whole truckload full of wormen
we didn't know if they's wives or daughters
most of them young and pretty
so some of the guys on the crew got to slipping
down and taking the extrey ones out
in the bushes we all thot that was okay
he didn't seem to mind or notice
we was just passing through
anyway one day when we was about ready
to go on here he come with a bunch of his boys
they had chains and knives and guns
and he's walking under his umbrella
so he wouldn't get the heatstroke
we thot we's all dead
I was ready to sez to him I never screwt nobody
but nobody sed nothing
he walked around till he found 2 faces
he knew I heard later niggers sez we all look alike
to them if I'd known that then
they'd of had to shot me cause I'd of run
but he picked the right 2 and we just thot
they're dead what do we do now?
but he had his boys
take their clothes off and then bend them
over a car hood and tie their legs up to the front

axle and their hands to the other wheel
so they's all stretched out tight
by then we figgered they'd castrate them
or cut them up and eat them or something
but we was wrong
we looked and seen 3 or 4 of the big ones
stripping off and then they greased up
their peters with white-rose salve
by god they almost cornholed
them 2 poor men to death
and made us watch
I never seen something so horrible
them poor bastards was screaming for somebody
to shoot them and both bled out the ass
one of them I've heard is still crippled up
and shits all over hisself
cause his asshole don't work right
fucking around with the wrong people
just don't pay that's what we built
whorehouses and beer joints for

we went on and built the rest
of the line but by then I was getting sick
from all that shit I got inside me
it messed up my stomach real bad
to where I got to shitting and puking blood
they put me on the airplane in Alabama somewheres
and brought me home to have a looksee
I was in terrible shape they sed
mebic distribulatary or something
and put me in the hospital for a year and
cut all my guts out
they sed they took out 15 foot of guts
and most of my stomach

I was plumb eat up with that stuff
when I got out of the hospital
I only weight 96 pounds
they sed I probly wouldn't live
but I did though I wouldn't eat no hominies
or lye-water grits for nothing
they had to give me all this blood
from other people
cause I couldn't hold mine in
and I kept getting sicker I got worried
I knew some of the blood was nigger blood
I didn't mind that
people who worry about that's stupider'n hell
it don't make no different
but they sez I got nemic
and I was afraid from that blood
mebbe I got that sick-as-hell nemic
that niggers get and die of
but they sed no it was different
I shouldn't worry about that
but I did anyways
I just couldn't help it

now I see up there
we already in Paragonah
I told you we'd get here
I think mebbe we better stop at your place
we're about out of beer
besides I'm about to pee all over myself
we got some time
I mean it's all
different now we didn't have

to get in all that trouble to have a little
fun back then we just made
our fun. Yep I miss them
times. I would of *never* dreamed
a womern could piss that far.

Back to the Valley

I guess mebbe you better be getting me home
now it's getting pretty late
and I'm getting pretty drunk
and tired
I got to get back on that swoker tomorrow
and cut hay the bank
he don't give much of a damn
as to whether I'm having a good time
or not he just wants his money on time
sometimes I think
if I gotta come back and wear out
another life like them Chinermens sez you do
mebbe I be the bank this time
I know it'd be bout my turn
and mebbe his to let me hold the deeds
just oncet
anyways that don't matter now
we got plenty of time
to worry bout that tomorrow
but I better get home and get some sleep tonight
so mebbe we better head on back

you know over yonder in them hills
LaVerne's brother he found a Indin grave oncet
it was a long time ago he wasn't very old yet
and he thot he'd just dig that grave up
to see if there's any jewelry or arrowheads or other
Indin shit in there with that feller
so he come back to it one day
with a shovel and started digging
he wasn't very far along when he sez he felt
sorta nervous like he's about to pee

or something but he knew he didn't need to
he'd arredy had on the way
so's he went on and then got another feeling
like somebody's watching him dig so's he stops
and turns around and there's a Indin standing there
right behind him wearing them Indin clothes
like they don't wear no more
you know them leggings and that thing over
their chest and all and moskins
LaVerne's brother he bout shit
cause he never heard nobody walk up
and he sez for a minute he couldn't say nothing
he just set there and finally he sez
what do you want? but that Indin
didn't say nothing just stood looking at him
and he sez I sez what do you want?
do you want me to leave? and when
he sed that that Indin just disappeared
right in front of him and never sed nothing
LaVerne's brother he was ascairt
he got the hell out of there
and won't go back though he told me
about it and it happened up there
somewheres in them hills behind
that old mill I don't know for sure just where
I wouldn't go there for anything
I aint gonna fool around with that stuff

I heard about 2 men out hunting deer
in the hills that got lost
and it started snowing so's they had to
hunt around for a place to get in
and found this cave and when they went in
it's all this Indin stuff

jugs and arrows and jewelry and stuff
and they had to spend the night in there and
they sez it's all haunted cause they heard
noises all night and couldn't sleep
so's when light come they filt their pockets
with all that shit they could carry and left
and finally found their ways home
but later they tried to come back and
get the rest of that stuff in the cave
cause it was worth money
but they looked all over and couldn't find it
again but they sez it's out there
and somebody'll find it one day
it aint gonna be me
I aint going in no haunted cave
for all the Indin jewelry in Chiner
it aint worth it to mess around
with no Indin ghosts
you just don't know what they might do

I aint talking about that no more
cause I get ascairt and then feel damn stupid
for doing it a grown man talking
about ghosts and stuff
oh I know they real I aint saying that
they just aint nothing I can do about them
and I aint for sure what they can do
about me so I just leave them alone
they was a haunted house back home
I was in and it made your hair stand up
on your neck when you walked in
didn't nobody have to tell you
you just knew something was wrong when you
walked in and you couldn't get a nigger

to go in that house for money
or whiskey and you couldn't thow
a cat through that house's door
it'd scream like hell and find someways
to keep from going in
cats and niggers they can tell things like that
that's why I won't have no damn cat around
they might just bring that stuff with them
I trapped a cat oncet or he got in my trap
I never planned it I wouldn't set no trap
for a cat and I was ascairt to kill him
he might come back or bring something in
so's I just forgot about that trap for a month
and when I got back surenuff he's dead
but it wasn't my fault
I won't kill no cat but that's how haunted
that house was and I don't
much like thinking about it even now

here I caint get the top screwt off
this beer can you hep?
that's the onliest thing I miss this finger for
I got cut off I just haven't got no grip
to twist off these beer lids
they put them on too tight for me now

they was this guy I heard about
who was a miner or trapper or something
anyways he lived alone up in the hills
he got his finger chopped off
I guess mebbe he's a trapper and got it
caught that happens now and then
so he just picked up his finger and stuck it
in his pocket and went on home

when he got there he took out his needle and thread
and he sewed that finger back on
his hand but it didn't work
2, 3 weeks later it all swoled up
green and the finger fell off
so's he built a fire in the stove
and then held the stump agin it
till he burnt all the green poison out
I think a feller'd have to be
pretty much of a man to do that

I knew this other guy who was loading up
a sow hog and she wouldn't go
so's he was trying to waller her into the truck
and he grabs her by the tail with
one hand and the ear with the other
she's screaming like hell the whole time
and him getting pretty pissed off
so's he does this a time or 2
and then he grabs her again but
gets the one hand in her mouth
he feels something pinch so
he pulls back his hand
and his finger's gone that damn sow's
bit him off he looked all round
and didn't find that finger nowhere
he guessed that sow swallered it

I don't much like to talk about how I lost
mine it still bothers me some
mebbe I'm just too drunk but I started thinking
about it. This all happened before
I went to work for the lectric company
I was younger and hired on for the oil

oh I made good money and it wasn't bad work
I don't think I'd do it again
anyways we's in Texas up on that panhandle
and had a rig drilling about 8 mile
outa town. We'd work 36 on and 12 off
at least I would cause I could make so much
I'd run chain awhile and then crow-nest
it never made no different
I was just after the paycheck on Fridays
I'd do bout anything they wanted as long
as the money kept coming in and they
seemed to like that
so anyways we was down over a mile
damn near 7 fousand foot
and we knew the oil was right there
we had to be coming thu any time
you just get the feeling it's gonna blow
so here comes the foman cause we sent for him
cause he has to sez when we can cap off
to get ready for the last push thu
so we don't blow all to hell and mebbe catch fire
that foman he's so goddam drunk
he caint tell shit from dog puke
he starts raising all kind of hell saying
you get this damn rig running right NOW
we won't hit no fucking oil
for 2 weeks nobody paid you to think
that's what I'm by god paid for
you just drill till I say stop and then
you just ast how long that's all
now git back to goddam work and stop
trying to set round fucking off
he left and we's so mad we couldn't see straight
for a man to talk to us that way

whether he's drunk or not didn't matter
so we set the bit back down in the night
and let her go wot the fuck
and about midnight the crewboss he sez to me
John you go up to the crow-nest we lifting
that pipe out I aint getting blowed up
for nobody and that was fine by me
we's all getting scairt to where we's just working
and not saying nothing just thinking
bout how long fore morning or till we got off
it's funny how you think the day'll take
the being scairt away but it never really does
anyways I climbt up the derrick to the top
and we's getting ready to pull that pipe out
when all of a sudden the whole thing starts shaking
to where I'm bout to get slung off
and I can hear the crewboss yelling
get down get DOWN this fucker's gonna blow
by god I burnt the palms off my hands
coming down I slid the wire guy rope
to the platform and then jumped off on the ground
the rest of the crew's arredy running ahead
so's I try to catch up and then I hear
that big sonofabitch touch off K-BOOM
right behint me and caught on fire
it blew me down on the ground and started
me burning by god I was ascairt
I jumped up and started running and I'd of
burnt to death if this nigger hadn't grapt me
and thowed me down in this ditch and
put the fire out on my clothes
so's we look and that whole rig's burning
and we can see 2 guys from the crew laying
between us and the rig burning up

and we know they's dead and
the rest of us is burnt bad where we might die
the crewboss he takes off running
into the fire and we can see he's gonna
try to bring the pickup out
he goes to it and grabs the doorhandle
and it's so hot part of his hand
sticks to the door and just comes off
but he gets in and somehows
he gets that damn truck started and drives out
of that fire I won't never know how
all the wires was burnt up
it got so hot that that truck's paint was all
scorcht off to where you couldn't tell even
what kind of a truck it was
and he brings it to us and we get in
I'm so burnt they had to put me in the back
and I'm laying in this feller's lap
who put out the fire in my clothes
and we pull out of there driving like hell
to get to town and by then the fire
was so hot it burnt up the whole goddam rig
there wasn't nothing left and I
seen it bend over just like it was plastic
I wanted to pass out so bad I couldn't stand it
but I didn't I just laid there and felt it all
and saw it all so's we're going to town
as fast as we can go and we pass this law
and he turns on his red light and chases us
till he gets close to see and then
he pulls ahead and leads us thu town
about 90 mile a hour to the hospital
where he jumps out and runs over and opens
the door and he just puked like hell

3 up front was arredy dead 2 of them
stuck together they's burnt so bad
and the crewboss's hand was off and he
didn't have no face left
how he drove God knows I don't
and there was only one other still alive and
he died that night so then they come
to get us out of the back and they started to lift me
out I sez get him first he saved my life
the man sez it's too late he's done dead
and I was laying in his lap

the onliest 2 that made it was me and
the crewboss. He was in the hospital for
96 days and I was in for 104
a week and a day more
I member cause he come to see me
when they let him out
he was burnt so bad I couldn't tell
who he was till he sed something
he ast if I's okay and I sed yas
we just looked at each other for a minute
and then he walked off
I sez be seeing you but he just waved
3 days later he drove his car
into a bridge and killed hisself
they buried him exactly one week after they
let him out and then let me out
the next day after his funeral was over

I don't have no bad scars left that show
my legs is burnt good
but I still feel it I get cold
and have to wear them long underwears

all year long on my legs
and my hands is so thin they bleed easy
my skin's bout as thick as a cigarette paper
and I don't have no feelings in my face
but I'm lucky I guess
all the rest is dead cept me

I went back to work for the oil
the next day because I didn't have nothing
else to do and they put me on chain
wrapping the pipes and that's when I done it
I hadn't been working a hour
when this feller on the other side
thew his chain and I felt it hurt
so's I finished and took off my glove
and the finger stayed in
I sez you sonofabitch you done
cut my finger off but I don't think
he heard he didn't say nothing
well I had it I went to
the man and sez that's it pay me off
oh he tried to get me to stay on
but I lost the taste
and didn't care no more

it was after that I went down South
and got my stomach cut out and
then I come here to die
it was a pretty place and I didn't have nothing better
ever day LaVerne'd pack me a lunch and
I'd draw her a map of where
I'd be if I didn't make it home
I was weak and couldn't hardly
stand so I'd drive up in the hills

where I'd take off my clothes
and let the sun shine on me
the muscles wouldn't heal up
on my stomach where I'd been burned
there was just ugly skin there you could see thu
I only weight 96 pounds and I'd lay
on a quilt and look back at the valley
and just wait to be dead and have it done

you know by god I guess I'd still
be laying up there waiting
cept after awhile LaVerne she went
and bought these 2 hogs for me
she knew I'd like that
I got to coming down early to feed them
and when I was up there
I'd get to thinking about the market
and making money
I got so cited I come down one day early
and went to looking for a boar
to get a herd started
and the next day I forgot to go up to die
then pretty soon I bout quit
thinking about it altogether
it just don't take much to keep
some people going

and that gets us about to here
which is nearly home
time for one last beer
they say God takes special care
of children and idiots
I guess he's been watching out for me

by god I'll always member them times
they was good times for the most
but I do hope to Christ they
don't never ever come back

The Porcine Canticles

Barbed Wire

You just cut that sombitch right here
KARL KOPP, YARBROUGH MOUNTAIN

It aint no easy way
to find the endpiece of wore
oncet it's in the roll
you can pick it up bounced it round
like this or roll it
upside the barn hard
mebbe it'll pop out
most times not
don't cost nothing to try
it was this man back home
name Johnny Ray Johnston
a inventer
he invented this thing it could help
find the endpiece
and sent it off to Warshington

he had this brother
name Haroldwayne Johnston
a blind gospel preacher
he wasn't always
he's a mean sonofabitch young
all filt up with sin and equity
fighting raising hell
had three four of them girls
his age up to the doctor
all before he's called
it was this other brother
named Leonas Timothy Johnston

he never learnt to read
so he got a job with the highway patrol
got shot by a shiner
I seen that worefinder
it worked my brother he bought one
where'd them pliers go?
so Haroldwayne one day
he's out in this field
where the neighbors run his hogs
hiding in the shinery
shooting a pellet gun
to watch them squolt and run
I guess he was lessee
it was two years before he tried to heal
Mavis Tittle's one that died
of the toothache so he must of been twenty-four
goddam watch it
wore'll tear the hide right off
your hands you seen them gloves?

this storm come up a sudden
caught him out there
looking like a cyclome
he had to get home so he run
by the time he got to the fence
it was hailballs coming down
he tried to climb through with the gun
poached hisself
shot right up his nose
made all the blood go in his eyeballs
he's blind
that fence caught him
he's straddled of one wore
the top one had him grapt by the butt

here comes the storm
he sez he could feel that wore
go green when the lightening struct
made him a eunuch
he could look right at a naked womern
wouldn't nothing go down
nor come up after that
you find them pliers? look
in the jockey box or under the seat
sez he heard God call him

he'd been hollering like a sonofabitch
they heard all the way to the house
and was fixing to come but he quit
they waited till it quit raining
sez they'd of thought he's dead
and that would of made two
only one brother left for a seed crop
all that blood out his nose
except he's praying to hisself out loud
he never even heard them come up
it isn't none there? look
in the back see if it's some sidecutters
or something so they known he'd got religion
and they never seen he's even blind yet

he's a gospel preacher after
and Johnny Ray's a inventer
Leonas Timothy was arredy shot dead
what it was was a piece of wore
it could be fixed on the end at the store
except it was red paint on it
wherever the red was was the end
when you's through using wore

then fix the red one on
next time there'd be the endpiece red
Haroldwayne he saved hundreds of lostsouls
come all over to hear him heal
best on headaches and biliousness
it was one family had this crippled boy
come about eighty miles to see him gospel preach
brung this boy up front
he taken and grapt his head
hollers the words and sez now walk
but he fell on his ast still crippled
they sez it wasn't Haroldwayne's fault
them people didn't have no faith
I heard he drownt a year or two after that

the govament never did send Johnny Ray
no patent agreement we figgered
he kept the invention for hisself
so Johnny Ray he made some up
and sold to his friends around town
you caint buy it nowhere else
I wisht I had one now
I've wasted more damn time on wore today
than I have to lose
bring them pliers here
let's cut this sonofabitch it don't matter where
we gone set here all day
won't never get this damn fence done

The Hay Swather

Dave John sez Dave is that you?
I sed hello John
John sez it's that damn swoker I bought
I sed did something go wrong arredy?
John sez yas so I sed but you just got it
it shouldn't break down that quick
was it bad? Goddam John sez
it busted all to hell
the manifold bushings mebbe a flywheel bearing
it could of been the drive shaft or cam I dunno
I tried to fix it and climbed underneath and beat it
with the hammer so when I went to start it up
the clutch jerked a knot in hisself
and felt across the ground
I had a hundred more acres of hay I told him
I'd knock down before weekend
and I didn't even have a dog with me
to kick his ast
it wasn't nothing I could do but stand and watch

I sed John I don't know anything
about machinery John sez whar?
I sed nowhere
John sez oh well that don't matter now
so I sed that's good
John sez if I could of found him I'd of
loosen up his hide right now
I sed whose? John sez
the one that solt me the swoker who you talking about?
I sed oh him
John sez yas but it was too late
so's I went home and made up these words

I practiced what to say in the night
next morning I got my truck and drove
to the crossroads before I got there I stopped
and put some of the words on my hand
so's I wouldn't be lost when I got mad
and if I hit him I'd have them all right there
he'd know how come
cause he was gone say well John I be damn
I'm sorry but it was a used one and all
there aint nothing he can do

I pulled up and he's standing right there
eating a sandwich for breakfast
and sez hello John I sez I gotta talk to you
right now he sez you want a sandwich
he hadn't had his breakfast yet
I sez no I aint got no time to eat a sandwich
I'd eat a cupcake and a can of Viennies
on the way so he sez come in
we went in his office and set down
I lain my hand out on the table so's I could
see the words I sez listen here
that swoker you solt me done busted all to hell
and it aint been that long
and you ought to do something about it
it aint right that way
I didn't say or I'll whup your ast
but I had it wrote down
if I needed it for later

he didn't say nothing
he picked up the phone I thot he's calling
the law mebbe but he sez Roy
tell Bubba unload that big truck to somebody

and he sez yeah now
I'll need it this morning so's he hangs up
the phone he sez John well
it's only one thing I can do
we'll go load up my swoker and take it out
to your place so's you won't lose no time
and load yours up and I'll bring it back
and fix her up cause I guaranteed it
all I sell for ninety days
if it busted reckon it's my fault not yours
so what else can I do for you this morning?

I sed John what'd you say?
John sez I looked at my hand
and I aint wrote nothing for that
so I sez that sandwich sounds fine
it's all I could think of
and I wasn't even hungry
I couldn't shake his hand
cause he might see them words I put on it
I never thought he'd go and say
something like that
and I couldn't just set there
so he torn his in half and we both
eat a piece waiting

Tuesday Morning, Loading Pigs

The worse goddam job of all
sez John pushing a thick slat
in front of the posts
behind the sow in the loading chute
so when she balked and backed up
she couldn't turn and get away
I never seen a sow or a hog load easy
some boars will
mebbe it's because they got balls
or something I don't know
but I seen them do it
that Brown feller the FFA
he's got this boar he just opens the trailer door
he comes and gets in
course he mebbe knows what
he's being loaded up for

it was this Ivie boy back home
the best I ever seen for loading
he wasn't scared of nothing
he'd get right in and shove them up
he put sixteen top hogs
in the back of a Studebaker pickup
by hisself I seen it
when he was a boy he opened up
the tank on the tractor
smelling gas
made his brains go soft they sed
he failed the fifth grade
but it wasn't his fault
he could load up hogs

I always had to at home
cause I was the youngest
I sed then it was two things
I wouldn't do when I grown up
warsh no dishes or load up hogs
by god they can set in the sink
a month before I'll warsh them
a man's got to have a principle
he can live his life by is what I say
now you grab her ears and pull
I'll push from back here
we'll get that sonofabitch in the truck

Tuesday Morning,
Driving to the Auction in Salina

Sometimes sez John
it's so pretty here I caint stand it
I'm on that hay swoker
it's green alfalfa all in front
and then them red Utah hills behind
climb up to the mountains
just like they're pasted on blue

but then it's times I'm alone I listen past it all
I hear Misippi
like a big muscle holding its blood
and the slosh on them rotten piles
down behind the house at night
I can almost see
that moon trying to push up the sky
reflected off the water
and the clouds fall apart
like pieces of paint
coming off old walls in the bedroom
it's almost the taste of fog
floating down the river
behind the cold nightwind
you know what I mean?

and John drove in silence
thinking me asleep
as I stared out toward the shrouded river
a thousand miles distant
listened to the sliding brown water

move over the etched memory
of a red-and-white bobber
dancing on the ripples of my mind

The Chain Letter (An American Tragedy)

Ohdammit sez John I'm in trouble
so I sed why John?
John sez I got the bill for my insurance
and I haven't got no money to pay it
cause I won't get paid for swoking and bailing
Keith Guymon's hay till next week
I done told him that would be just fine
when he ast a week ago but
LaVerne she went and opened the damn envelope
on a chain letter and I aint got no time
to write out twenty copies
I got to get that hay finished
so what am I posta do now?

I sez what John? John sez
it's the damn govament
sends them things out I know it
and it works with the post office and
the insurance to keep you in line
I sez what John?

John sez my brother oncet
he got this chain letter back home
he didn't have no time
to write out his copies neither
it sez he has four days to wrote it
before the luck comes good or bad
it aint never good I heard of
but he forgot
back then it was $5,000 this feller got
in four days and then later
when the govament ruint the money

he put on a zero it was $50,000
and then it was $100,000
now it sez he got $420,000
it's the same guy it was in
that letter back then
just the numbers changed
it's the way the govament has
to let us know how much
he's gone let the money be worth
but the next day because he hadn't
wrote out his twenty letters
he lost all that money
but my brother he was busy too
he didn't do his letters

the third day after
he had to go kill these pigs
for this man but this other feller
was gone bring his milkcow down
get her bred to my brother's bull
he told him go ahead and do it
he sez he'd have his boy
walk her down the road
it wasn't far
so while my brother was gone
his boy brought her down
turnt her in the corral
he climbt up on the fence to watch

it might of been fine
except the hogs been rooting
up under the barn wall
my brother he borrowed
this lectric fence

he strung it along the side of the barn
so the bull mounts up on the milkcow
she turns and backs him up
against the barn he's stuckt
he gets his back feet
tangled in that lectric fence
one in front and one back
he tries to move and he just tightens
up the lectric wire
that boy he sez you could hear it
zzip zzip zipp that bull
he starts to bellering
milkcow she don't know
what's going on so she backs him up
tighter against the barn
it isn't no way he can get off
he commences to jumping up and down
on her and trying to get his feet
loost of that lectric wire
but he caint it goes zzip
he bellers and she backs up more
it goes zzip again
it was like he was doing a dance
like them crazy people do
trying to get his legs loost
hollering like a sonofabitch

so it was hogs there too
they heard it and here they come
it wasn't natural and a hog
it won't let nothing that's not natural
stay that way around them
it has to get right or go away or die
that boy sez they all run up

grunted and squolt like hell
when that didn't work
this one old mean bitching sow
she run right in between them
she bit that bull right on his seeds
she wanted him to stop acting that way
making all that noise
jumping up and down like that
right now

that bull he just went over backwards
right up against the barn
like he'd been shot in the head
knocked the whole goddam end
of the barn down
fell right on his back
the end rafter come down
on his chest it torn a piece of skin off
his pecker to his seeds
wide as your hand
they swolt up like basketballs
from the hogbite
broke ribs they figured
but it never did kill him
that milkcow she wasn't finished
she kept backing up
and fell down right on top of him
it was only the end of the barn
come down the rest stood up
that boy he's ascairt
he got his daddy's milkcow up
off my brother's bull he left
he sed he seen enough for oncet

my brother that night
he's coming home from killing them hogs
he never knew none of this happened yet
he's driving see? and he'd lost
his picking finger on his left hand
in the leaf springs of a wagon
when we's kids so
he's driving left-handed
and doing the gears and picking
with his right hand
it was a moon out so he'd turned off
his pickup lights listening
to the radio because his battery
wasn't much good
he couldn't do both
while he was driving
he couldn't see good as
he thot he could
he hit this big chuckhole
slung him right into the steering wheel
he figured it would of broke his nose
if he hadn't been picking
but his hand took the cushion
it only give him a nosebleed
but almost broke his hand
where it hit
his knuckles was bruised so bad
he couldn't even open and shut
his fingers for a week
he had to drive the rest of the way home
left-handed and lean acrost
and shift with that hand too
he thot the other one was broke
but it wasn't

he got home and the first thing
he seen was the end of his barn out
that bull standing there
inside the barn with his head down low
my brother thot he'd butted it down
he run in the house to get his gun
he was mad he would of kilt that bull
but they told him how it happened
so he didn't
he went out to look
but it wasn't no way they could
get that bull to go back in that yard
where them pigs was
he wouldn't go out the barn
they hit him acrost the butt
with a board he'd just stand there
he didn't care no more

they went in the house
my brother he got out the dishpan
and soaked some cold water
so he lain his hand in it
to get the swollen to go down
he wouldn't tell them how it happened
at first but while he was setting there
with his hand ducked
he remembered that chain letter
he jumped up and run to get it
sloshed water all over the kitchen floor
he was hollering how long's it been?
how long's it been?
they sez it happened this morning
it was just this morning
he sez whar? they sez when the sow

bit the bull on his seeds
knocked the barn down
he hollers no not that
how long's it been since I got
this here chain letter in the mail?
they sez oh three days
he sez goddam I only got one day left

my brother he set up all night
writing out his twenty copies
he had to tape the pencil to his hand
cause it was swole up
his fingers wouldn't bent
they sed he even wrote some
with his left hand
it was so bad you couldn't read the words
he got them all done by sunup
the fourth day like it sed
and took it to the mailbox

he waited all morning on the porch
till they remembered it was Memoral Day
the mail he wouldn't come
my brother he about had a worm
he run out to the mailbox
and got them letters he run over
to his pickup and clumb in
it wouldn't crunk
he'd run the battery down
listening to the radio
goddam my brother he was mad
he busted the side winder
with his head when that pickup
wouldn't turn over

jumped out and slammed the door
so hard it didn't catch
it bounced back and hit him
right on his swole-up hand
it hurt so bad he sez
he nearly fainted of the pain
he knew he had to get them letters
in the mail
so he walked all the way to town
it was more'n ten miles back then
it worked
nothing else happened
they got the end back in the barn
without it coming down
but they had to shoot the bull finally
and eat him
because he wouldn't do nothing
just set there and waste away
he'd seen enough they guessed
it wasn't no way he'd go
back out there with them pigs
in the corral

since then ever time
we seen a envelope in my family
it looks like it might be a chain letter
we don't open it till we got time
to set down right then
and make out them twenty copies
like it sez to do
but this time LaVerne must of forgot
it snuck up on her
when I got home it was laying
on the table and it wasn't nothing

I could do
it was my name on the envelope

I know it come from the insurance company
it was two years ago the man's wife
from the insurance called
she sez to LaVerne then that she wanted her
to come to her house
she wanted to tell her about selling Amway
LaVerne she sez she wasn't inarrested
a week later here comes
the insurance bill
by god it's gone up almost double
I sez how come you didn't go?
you could of just set and nod
now see what happened?
but it was too late

so I'm gone have to stay up tonight
writing chain letters
I done wrote one to send to the insurance
so he'll know I did it
and let the govament know
I wrote him a note on the bottom
and sez I'll pay the insurance bill
as soon as I can
but things is tough all over
I just hope he'll understand
I'd as soon right now
rather not have no luck at all
but I am willing to cooperate
if that's what my duty is
as a patriotic American citizen

The Muffler and the Law

1

You got a sow in heat? John sez
this morning when he called
I sed oh yas John I got four right now
John sez it wouldn't one
be that big black one would it?
I sed yas she's in I'm going to turn her
in with the boar this afternoon
John sez I'll be right down
to get her I want to borrow that sow
he hung up

John brought his beat-up truck
to my house with his big spotted boar
loaded in the back and a partition
so another hog could be put in
but the boar couldn't get to it
he drove right out to my loading chute
by the time I got there
John was trying to load up my big black sow
I sed John what are you doing?
John looked at me like I was crazy
he sez you gone hep me or stand there?
I didn't say anything else
I helped John load up my big black sow
and John drove off with her
in his truck and never did say where

2

Late afternoon John drove up
to my house he honks

he yells Dave come hep me unload
this big black sow of yours
she's done bred
I don't need her no more
he drives out back
to the loading chute
and unloads the sow
before I can get there

                    3

John I sed what the hell's going on
I mean you come get my big black sow
drive off without telling me anything
and you bring her back bred
to your spotted boar
what if I didn't want her bred to him?
John sez no charge
so it was all right then
I was going to tell him he could take
the other three sows that were in
for a ride all day tomorrow if he wanted
but John shut the gate on his stockracks
and sat down on his tailgate

it was this deputy sheriff
John sez so I sed which? John sez
that one in Richfield
last week going to the auction at Salina
I run over this rockslide
on the cutoff by Cove Fort
I busted my muffler pipe loost
and all the brackets I had to stop
on the summit and fix it all up
with bailing wire

it took a hour almost and I was late
for the auction so I had to go
the muffler was loost
and it made noise
but I didn't have no more time
I had to hurry

I got to Richfield
here comes this law
his red lights on and his siren honking
right in the middle of town
I got out and sez I'm late to the auction
he slams his car door and put his hand
on it he puts his other hand right down
on his gun sez I don't know whar
you from mister but in *my* town
we got a law here
I'm standing there with a truckload of hogs
people driving by slow looking at me
right in the middle of Richfield
I sez I'm late to the auction again
what I done wrong this time?
he sez in my town we got a law
against loud mufflers so you gone have
to pay you a fine for it mister
I sez look I done hit this rockslide
coming and busted
I tried to wire it up but couldn't
you look under here you can see
I'm late to the auction
his red lights was still going

I bent down to show him the wire underneath
he jumped in his car and taken out

his microphone he called this other law
so I stood up he sez you stand right there
I sez whar? he sez right there
he jumps out his car and puts his hand
on his gun again sez you trying
to resist arrest on me
I sez no I'm trying to show you
the bailing wire under here
holding up the pipes and the muffler
where I hit the rock on the mountain
but I caint hold the muffler on right
and the auction starts in fifteen minutes
he sez you just stand right there still
I got a reaforcement coming
we gone arrest you

4

I sed what happened John? John
sez the other law he come
and they both wrote me out a ticket
for loud mufflers and resisting arrest
and the other one that come
sez he believed I was speeding too
but they never wrote a ticket for it
and that's too bad cause I was
I was late for the auction

I sez can I go now? but the law
he sez you got to pay your fine
I sez the auction started five minutes ago
and I got to get there
the other law he sez why you
going to the auction you selling hogs?
I never sez a word to that dumb sonofabitch
he's standing right there by my truck

loaded up with twelve top hogs
wallering each other in the middle of town
all the cars driving by watching
the first law sez you got to foller us
to the JP I sez isn't it no other way?
he sez you trying to bribe a officer of law?
I sez hell no I'm trying to get to the auction
the other law sez whar?
and the first sez Salina they sell hogs at one
I sez that was ten minutes ago
the other law sez you selling these hogs?
but I wasn't talking to him
the law sez you want a regular judge
you can come back next Friday
but the fine goes up for that
I sez can I go now? and the law sez yas
but the other one sez not till you
get that muffler fixed

I had to get my truck towed
to a filling station four blocks away
and the muffler pipe welted
he charged me forty-seven dollars
and sixty-five cents to do it
I could of done it for a dollar
at home if I had my tools
by then the auction was over
I had to drive all them pigs home
after I'd loaded them up that morning
to take to the auction at Salina

5

I sed that's too bad John
John sez I couldn't sleep about it

for a man to talk to me that way
all he had to done was look
under the truck so he could see
it wasn't my fault
I tried to fix it best I could

he sez the fine would go up
so I sez to myself John it's done costed
fifty dollars almost so you
might as well get your say out of it
but I didn't have no sow in heat
so that's how come I called you

I sed John I don't understand
John sez I drove to Richfield
with that panel between the hogs
my spotted boar he about chewed it
in two trying to get your big black sow
but he couldn't so I went right to the spot
where that law pulled me over
in the middle of town
I stopped my truck and got out
climbed up on my stockracks
I took out the panel
let the boar go to her

I sed you did what? John sez
by god she wasn't quite ready yet
she squolt and here come the cars to see
I bet they could hear her half a mile
then here come the law
with his red light on
he sez what in the hell are you doing?
I sez here I am to pay my fine

he sez you get that truck out of here
with them pigs people's watching
I sez whar? he waved his arms he sez
everwhar see them they all coming
I sez I got to pay my fine I come to go
to court he sez whar? I sez right here
lord it was horrible my spotted boar
he slobbered all over your black sow
it was hog slobber on both her ears
that law he's as red in the face
as a fox's ass he couldn't do nothing
he finally sez you get your truck
you foller me I sez that's fine
but go slow I got a load of hogs in mine
I caint be jostling them any
we drove to the courthouse

6

Judge he sez what's going on?
law he sez you honor he's disturbing peace
Judge he sez how? law he sez
he's got these pigs in his truck
and they copperlating in the middle of town
Judge he sez whar? law he sez
right out there so Judge gets up
he looks out his winder there's my truck
by now my spotted boar he's done
he lain down and wasn't getting up
pooped Judge sez all I see is a hog
law he sez but they was scruting!
Judge he sez don't you talk that way
in a court of law you hear me?
all I see is a hog and it isn't no law
that sez this man caint haul no hog

through town in his truck yet
we haven't passed that law yet
so I sez you honor I want you to listen
to my side of this so I told him
the whole story about the muffler
and the law how I missed the auction
he looks at that law he sez
is it the way it happened like he sez?
law he commenced to squirming
but he has to say yassir you honor finally
I told him how it costed me fifty dollars almost
to get it fix and I had to be towed
four blocks with twelve top hogs in the truck
Judge he sez case dismissed and he sez
to me he's sorry about it all
specially the fifty dollars so I sez it's the way it is
caint be nothing done now
I didn't have no more hard feelings
so we shaken hands and I left

law he's mad as hell outside waiting
he sez mister you ever come to my town
again I'll make you sweat I'll
arrest your ass and thow you in jail
I sez mister deputy sheriff law
you listen here you listen good
you ever bother me again for anything
next time I'll pull a trailer and bring
eight sows and three boars all together I'll park
in front of the schoolhouse and take out the panel
I'll go in and tell them you sez for me
to meet you there and where are you
you posta have the money for me for them hogs
if you don't believe it you just try

and I sez then so you just get out of my way
I walked on past him and went and left
he never sez one more word to me

7

so here's your big black sow
John sed and he stood up
she's done bred to my spotted boar
but you don't owe me nothing
I aint never won one with the law before
so I reckon this one's on me
John closed his tailgate and leaned in
and patted his spotted boar
on the head and then John got in
his beat-up truck and drove home for supper

Culture

So Aeneas walked up the Tiber until he found
a sow
she had a litter of thirty pigs
and he knew it was a sign
that would be the place

Where'd he go to get a boar?

No, it was a myth

But where'd he get his boar?

He didn't. He killed the sow on the site
and sacrificed
her to the gods for marking the place

You goddam stupid sonofabitch how come you telling me
stories like that I'm busy I haven't got no time to listen to
that horseshit you go get in your car and go on home and
find you another book to read and you tell him next time call
me I'll make it right with god and him both you tell him a
sow hog has thirty pigs I'll trade him my pickup straight
acrost sight unseen but I don't want to hear it now I got
work to do who wrote that damn book he must of lived in
New York City his whole life in a whorehouse somewhere
just go on I aint listening to no more writing like that I don't
need it you tell him if he doesn't know nothing about pigs
then don't write about pigs he should find something else
that's all

The Real Estate

for Herbert Scott

Has them real estate been bothering you?
sez John I sed no John
not that I know of John sez
he been after me
ever since they opened that gravels pit
down by my pigpens
he calls up he sez is this John Sims?
I wondered who the hell he thot I'd be
he called up my number
but I sez yas he sez well this is
the real estate and I love to list up
your pigpens for sale
cause I done have it sold for you

I sed what'd you say John?
John sez I sez no that's whar
my pigs is if I sold my pigpens
them pigs wouldn't have no place to be
the real estate he sez well John Sims
you could buy another place to put my pigs
he sed he already had a place picked out
so I sez whar? he sez out by Lund
I sez that's twenty-five miles away
he sez but he can make me a good price
I sez it isn't no water out there
and I aint hauling no fucking water
he sez but it isn't no water at my pigpens
I sez to him them's only down the road
I can haul it that far
he sez it isn't any either place

so what's the different? I sez twenty-five miles
down and then back is the different
caint you add? he sez well
John Sims you think about it
cause I done got a buyer for your pigpens
he hung up before I could tell him
I didn't have no time to think
I had to cut hay today

I sed John that's that you don't have to sell
anything you don't want to
he won't bother if you make it clear
John sez he done call me back
three times a week for a month
he sez well John Sims I done took
earnest money on them pigpens
when can you get your hogs moved?
I sez I told you twicet arredy no
this week how come you keep calling me?
he sez them gravels need that land
to park his trucks on
I sez my pigs lives there he sez
well John Sims I done took care of that
he told that one at Lund I sez yas
I'd buy that piece of ground there
without no water to build pigpens
twenty-five miles from my house on
I sed John don't let him do that
don't sign anything he can't make
you sell anything you don't want to

John sez they done done this before
it was this aunt my cousin had
that lived in Oklahoma

she had this farm the real estate wanted
to make a graveyard out of
because it was next door
and got full but she sez no
they call her up all the time sez
Mizrez Scott we done got to have that farm
for the graveyard but she wouldn't sell
so they quit cept after that
she'd hear all this noise at night
scratch on her winders
and it was dogshit in a sack
on her porch on fire
she'd get it on her shoes
stomping the fire out
she called the sheriff he sez well
Mizrez Scott you taken and buy
you a shotgun for it but you
don't go outside or he can sue you
it has to be breaking in

two years she set up nights
with that shotgun
she'd hear noise at the winder she'd
shoot it and the insurance sed he wouldn't help
it was costing her eighty dollars a month
to shoot her winders
oncet it was the milkcow
she shot out its eye
it didn't die but she sed
it dried up and she had to sell it
at the auction anyway

two years after one night
she never heard nothing she sed

she seen something outside
so she shot the winder out
a little later it was this knock
on the door so she opened it up
this man standing there shot
she hadn't saw before
blood all down his shirt
he wasn't dead he sez
how come you shot? I aint scratched
the winder yet you posta wait
till I scratch then shoot
she had to drive him to the hospital
to get them buckshots took out
his shoulder and he told the sheriff
the real estate done paid him
to scratch her winder to scare her off
but the real estate sez they couldn't prove it
they had to let him go
Mizrez Scott was eighty then

I sez that's too bad John sez
she died after that and the real estate
got the county to take the farm
he bought it from the county
and then sold half of it back to them
for twicet what he'd paid them
for the graveyard and kept the rest
cause he was on the commission
I sez that's too bad John
there ought to be laws for that

John sez I caint haul no water
twenty-five miles I'm gone have to buy
that piece of ground next to my place

to put my pigs on
I sed why John? you don't have to sell
your pigpens John sez
I called the gravels man last week
he sez go to hell the real estate
he given me four fousand dollars
for my pigpens and sed he'd help me
move the pigs to a new place
I can buy that piece next door
that has water for that
what am I posta do then?

I didn't say anything so John sed
I caint have the real estate paying no man
two years to scratch on my winders
so I can shoot them out
I have to sleep at night
so I can cut hay in the daytime
wouldn't you? and I nodded yes
because John was right
for that price I would have sold
John's pigpens too

Mean

Hell Hath No Fury Like a Sow with Pigs

1

Pretty soon now I sed and
John nods his head watching
so I sed I see she's broken the sack
there's water and his head goes up and down
again but he doesn't say anything
so we both stand and watch
John's big white sow back in her shed
while she breathes easy
seven hundred pounds sprawled across yellow straw
finally John sez any time now
and I nod my head this time
he sez yep just any time
but the only thing we can do is watch
so we stand and wait
and watch John's white sow labor
and John lights a cigarette
to help the time go by while we watch

2

Last time sez John she went crazier'n hell
I had her in that pen with a wood floor
I put in a lamp for the cold and
she's half done and got up that mean sonofabitch
she done went over and bit that lectric wire
and it shocked her or something
she went like a crazy womern to banging
her head on the walls and floor
and hollered like a elephant shot in the butt

with buckshot she tore hell out of that pen
and had two more pigs while she's standing up and
never knew it she acted like she's blind
and couldn't see nothing I had to get
them pigs out with a rake or she'd of stomped
on them all she jerked that rake
right out of my hand twicet I had
to get it back with a stick so's I could get
them pigs out or they'd be dead
I got all but one that she killed
and she finally went over and lain down
to have her pigs again but ever time
one of them I had out squolt she'd jump up
and go crazy again I had to put them pigs
in the front of my pickup all night
to make her be still and that light
never did work after that she ruint it
so I sez how come you keep her John?
she's too big and mean and John
looks at me like I was nuts or something
he sed cause she had twelve pigs and raised
all but one more besides the one she stomped
that's why, wouldn't you? but I didn't
say anything, John's white sow was too mean
for me, I would have sold her to John
if she was mine but she wasn't
she was already John's so I didn't have to

    3

John I sez after awhile because she wouldn't pig
I'll bet that sow's got a pig stuck breech
and it won't come but John looks over
at his pickup and doesn't say anything
so I say if she does and it doesn't come

it could kill her and all them pigs too
don't you think? but he keeps looking at
his pickup so I say I don't know of course
but that might be it she's been in labor
a long time and she broke her water
before I got here I saw the last of the wet
when I came but I don't know she's not my sow
it might not be that but John sez real low
she throwed Carl out of the pen that time
he got in and tried to climb out after him
she'd of killed him if she'd got to him
so I decided I wouldn't say anything else
she was John's sow and he'd know what to do

4

Why don't you get in there and look
sez John you know more about that than I do
and I sez no I don't John and I have
to be getting home pretty soon Jan will be
getting worried and I hate to keep
her up John sez Dave I'll give you twenty-five
dollars if you'll go get that pig out and
I sez John I'm not getting in that pen with
that sow for a hundred dollars John sez
okay fifteen dollars cash I sez no John
I'm not going to get in there for a thousand
dollars John sez I'll give you a pig
I sez I wouldn't do it for the sow and all
the pigs loaded up to take to the auction
John sez okay a live pig and you can pick it
but I sed no and I meant it
not for all his pigs and I acted like I
was getting ready to leave
I wasn't I wanted to see how it came out
but I wasn't getting in that pen

so John goddammed me and sed I was a sissy
and I didn't say anything because John was right

5

John sez if I get in there will you come
and hold the lantern in the door so I can see?
and I sed yas because the sow was in
bad shape by then we could see that and
she had to have help but I sed John
if she comes after me I'm getting out
and I'm not going to worry about the lantern
getting out with me so it may get busted
John sez if she gets up you just make sure
you don't get in my way or she'll get you
and the lantern both and I sed okay
because I knew there's no way John
can get out of that pen before me
I wasn't worried about that
so I sed where's the lantern? John sez
over here so we go to his pickup
for the lantern and John gives me the lantern
and some clean rags to hold then
he gets in his jockey box and pulls out
a pistol I sez what's that? and John sez
it's a gun and I sez ohIsee and he sez
I aint getting in there with her without no
gun my mama didn't raise no idiots
and if I need this I want to have it
with me that's why and he put it in
his coat pocket and I didn't say anything
because it wasn't my sow she was John's

6

John climbed in the pen and I followed
he went in the shed with the sow but I
stayed in the door while he moved around
behind her slow to see what she'd do
she had her eyes closed and breathed
hard because she hurt so bad
and I shined the light in so John could see
John knelt down behind her and touched her
but she didn't move so he rolled up his sleeve
and started in to see what was wrong
breech? I whispered and he nodded so
I was right and John went in to try and get it out
John whispers hold still I caint see
and I sez who? and he sez you and
I saw the lantern was shaking I was scared
so I held it with both hands and it
was still John twisted his hand inside the sow
and he sed I got it I'm gone take it out now
he started pulling his arm back and the
pig came out and it was breech
got it? I sed and John sez yas gimme a rag
and I leaned in to hand him a towel and
the pig wiggled in his hand John tried to grab
its mouth but the pig squealed in his hand

7

Goddam you John screamed
the white sow jumped up and bellowed
so loud the tin roof on the shed shook
and jerked around toward John
I stood there like Lot's wife shining the light in
John screams goddam you again
and jumps back against the back wall

of the shed and hits it so hard it should have
come down holding the pig tight against his chest
the sow roars at him the muscles
in her body standing out all the hair on
her back straight up and I think drop that pig
John but I can't say anything I'm frozen
holding the lantern in the door
the sow roaring and John screaming
then he tears at his pocket and pulls out
the pistol goddam you he yells you get away from me
you sonofabitch and the sow barks loud like a maddog
the size of a jersey cow
John points the pistol at her head and it shakes
like an aspen limb in springtime
goddam you and she screams again
snick snick snick snick snick snick snick
I see the empty cylinder turn as John pulls
the trigger and I taste powder in my mouth
drop it! I hear somebody say
John keeps pulling the trigger yelling goddam you
the sow roars and her shoulders bunch up in a knot
she's so mad she's slobbering
DROP IT I yell again and John looks at me
his eyes wide as hubcaps
DROP THAT PIG I scream and I see John's
hand loosen and the pig falls to the ground
but he keeps pulling the trigger snicksnicksnick
the pig hits on its back and lies there
and the sow lowers her head and looks at it
but keeps on grunting loud and mean and fast
John stops pulling the trigger but keeps the pistol
pointed at her head and the pig gets up
and starts moving the sow quits grunting and
sniffs it then looks at John and barks again

John pulls the trigger again but he can't
say anything anymore and the sow turns and lies down
and grunts and another pig pops out
the first pig finds her and tries to find a teat
and the second pig squirms and shakes its head and
tries to clear its nose and John stands with
the pistol pointed at the sow and I stand
holding the lantern and the sow grunts to her pigs
just like we're not there and nothing happened
and I say John? and John points the pistol at me
I say get out John and he sez whar?
and I say get out of that shed John before
she gets up and John sez who? and I say
get out of there John and John looks at the sow
and points the pistol at her and he starts
sliding around the wall and we get out
of John's mean white sow's pen

8

John's shaking so hard he can't light
a cigarette so I do it but he drops it on
the floorboard and I pick it up and put it
in his mouth and he smokes
I say you got a beer? and he sez in the back
I think so I take the lantern and look
and he has some hid in his junk in the bed
I get it and for a long time we drink beer
and don't say anything and I see that my hands
are shaking so the beer foams out the top of my can
so I drink three fast so it won't
and I don't know if he ever finished his
finally I sed John I wouldn't have a pig like that
I'd get rid of her if she's mine she's just too mean
she's gonna kill somebody someday

John's staring straight ahead through the window
the muscles in his face still tight, drawn
he sez goddammit that's too bad
and I sed well you can't help it some go mean
he sez she was a good sow I sez she's okay now
John sez but it was her or me and I sez it's okay
he sips his beer then sets it on the dashboard
and leans back and I see tears in his eyes and
he's still staring straight ahead through the windshield
she was a good sow he sez even if she was mean
goddammit I hated having to shoot her like that
and I looked out the window and didn't
say anything. She was John's sow, not mine.

Friday Afternoon, Feeding Pigs

John I sed this guy told me
if you broke your leg and fell down
in a pigpen and couldn't get out
the pigs would eat you
do you believe that? John sez
he don't raise no pigs
the one that sed that story
did he? and I sed noIdon'tthinkso
John sez most of the people who sez
things like that don't or is wormen
that need something to say
those who do leave it alone

when I's young Eugene Cummings
fell down in his pigpen
and had a heart attackt
he's dead
so when they found him
it was afternoon
he'd gone out to feed his pigs that morning
his face was blue
when they turned him over
to ast him if he was alive or not
his eyes pooched out so
they made dents in the ground
where he lain
they sed you could of sawed them off
with a hacksaw
my brother was there he sed
R.B. McCravey he sez he'd of loved
to known what it was Eugene Cummings
was thinking about

that brung it on they sed
he chased around the young girls a lot
with his pickup truck in the evenings
mebbe he was daydreaming
seen a naked vision and couldn't
handle it I wasn't there
so I don't know I's too young back then
when Mama found out
she went over to Mizrez Cummings' house
to help out with the crying
she's a neighbor so she could
make her feel better and find out
whatall happened
how come his eyes was stuck out that way
she took me and I set in the corner
I was only about nine back then
listening and the wormen talked it out
Mizrez Cummings she never sed nothing
everbody knew they never slept
in the same bed at night
and hadn't for years she didn't care much
but had to act proper

one of them it was Mavis Tittle I think sed
it was a great issue of blood
that rose up and hit his brains
like a giant hailball come down from God
and struct his mind with power
he never felt a thing
I think she's lying the way they sez
his eyeballs was out he felt it
they all rocked in the furniture
and nodded to make her feel better
about only having to make up one bed

in the morning anymore
it was a bowl of red incarnations
on the table I remember somebody sent
that was pretty but Mizrez Cummings
she wouldn't look at them
I could tell she didn't want
to think about it that much

they buried him and I seen him
in his box at the funeral
you couldn't tell his eyes was pooched out
Rufus got them right
so he just looked dead
his family set together
his boy's girlfriend set by him
she worn this pointed bassiere
that made her look like she had
snow-cone cups under there
my brother he kept sighting across
the aisle at her
since it was a funeral
nobody paid him any attention
everbody else was looking at the family
or her too like you do then
to see how they're taking it

it was a new preacher at the churchhouse
he never seen Eugene Cummings before
but he lain it on
sez God he's calling in his folds
preacher talk we couldn't hardly understand
like they learn to do in preacher school
he went on for a hour
about God and heaven and the churchhouse

and the collection plate
how glorious Eugene Cummings was
now he's dead in his box
Mama sed oncet or twicet she wondered
if Mizrez Cummings would of liked
to of slipped up and seen who Rufus put
in that box the way that preacher
carried on but she never
I remember I's having a hard time
setting still that long
my brother he had a crick in his neck
the next day from looking across the aisle
at Eugene Cummings' boy's girlfriend's pointed bassiere
for such a time
Mama sed that young feller
he had his wick up so high
he sooted his chimley
but it finally got done and we left

at the graveyard we all shaken hands
after it was over
you'd go through the line and at the end
it was Rufus because he was in charge
him and the preacher
so my brother when he got up to him
he sez Rufus tell me something
did them hogs eat on him any?
Rufus sed not a bite
I heard it because I was right behind
my brother not a bite? he sez
Rufus sed nope not a mark on him
the preacher he had to say something too
so he sez the Lord carries on or somesuch
it never made any sense

but my brother didn't want to be polite
he didn't tell him so
we taken up his fingers and
shaken his hands and just left
he didn't ask Rufus how he got them eyes
mashed back in and I was too young to
so I never did find out
funeral people can do most anything
to a dead body they say and preachers
but you can tell your friend
it don't always happen that way
because Eugene Cummings lain there
the whole day and it was August
so it would of been hot
they'd of smelt him for sure
but his hogs never ate a bite of him
they just set in their mud and watched
cause Rufus sed so at the graveyard
and that's a fact

Building a Farrowing Pen

Hot sez John godamitey it's hot
we better drink a coldbeer
and set in the shade a minute
I sed okay because it was hot
and I was tired of building pigpens
so I went to the pickup and
got the beers while John
found a cool place to sit
where the breeze could cross us
John's stomach hurt where they'd cut
nine feet of amoebic dysentery out
he held himself
arms crossed in front
eyes closed, rocking
I sed hurt? but he didn't answer
rocked and worked his jaw
eyes tight

I was in Misippi John sez finally
we's stringing wore for the lectric
when I seen these wild dogs
people'd turned loose in the sloughs
running in this pack
when I seen them they's just standing there
watching me up on the pole
and I seen them watching
it wasn't nothing else to do but work
and watch out there alone so's I did
it helped the time pass

then they hired on Coy Stribling
Brother Coy Stribling but I wouldn't call him that

his eyes was so close together
he's almost looking out the same hole
he's the ChurchofGodofholyanddivineprophecyandrevelation
but it didn't matter they had to fire him
after about a week
he just couldn't catch on to nothing
he wasn't my brother
I couldn't stand it when he looked at me
cause of them eyes

one day it was this deer
run out in a clearing and his leg
was dragging back so I known
them dogs seen him if I did
here they come and drug him down
right out there in front of us
we set there and watched
it standing right there alive
a minute ago
he wasn't no more than down
them wild dogs torn open his guts
and back legs eating it

Coy Stribling he sidled me
he sez Brother John
he called everbody Brother something
whatall his name was
had his little red Gideon newtestament
they give his kids in the school that year
he kept in his pocket
out in his hand
he sez that there's a vision sent down from God Amitey
I almost sez oh bullshit Coy Stribling
it's dogs people turned loose

trying to find something to eat to
stay alive but I didn't
you caint do nothing for people like that
it's too late
with his eyes like that he needed
something to believe in
so I let it alone
he was standing and nodding his head
almost slobbering he believed it so

that deer raised his head
and looked back over his shoulder
watched them wild dogs eat it
saw pieces of his own belly tore off
and swallered and them wild dogs go back
for more me standing
out there a hundred yards off watching
it was like how a sow hog
when she's farreling hurts like a sonofabitch
getting them babies out her stomach
but she'll turn her head up
to look at them while she's doing it
you can see that same look
in her eyes and
it just lain its head down
and died
I was watching

Coy Stribling he never seen a thing
after them wild dogs took him down
he's talking to hisself and nodding
at his newtestament in his hand
it wasn't nothing else he could do

I set my beer on the ground
between my legs and saw the foam rise
John didn't say anything else
he lit a cigarette and smoked and
we sat in the shade and let the wind
blow over us while we rested
John's arms crossed in front
his head back against the pigpen
eyes up to the scraps of clouds
drifting north, rocking

The Farm

We sold it. To a man
who would be a patriarch.
I told John we were closed in,
subdivisions and trailers all around,
complaints of the smell (though
there was none), Ira came out
and told me to keep them fenced
(though none broke out), the neighbors
frightened because someone's cousin's
friend heard of a hog
that ate a child who fell in the pen (though
their children rode my sows
at feeding time), because I was tired,
because Jan carried our child and could
no longer help, because she wanted a home.

And the patriarch lost his first crop
to weeds, threw a rod in the tractor,
dug a basement and moved the trailer on
for extra bedrooms, cut the water lines
for a ditch, subdivided the farm
and sold the pigs for sausage. I told John
they were his, they were no longer mine,
I couldn't be responsible.

The wire connecting our voices was silent
for a moment. "You stupid sonofabitch," was all
he finally said. "You poor stupid bastard."

Aftermath

There were pigs
in the night, a wild herd
overran the farm, trampled
my fences and flowers, rooted the garden.
Lost in the depths of overturned garbage cans,
their grunts echo the darkness
as they search the land
while the night reaches out before them
like a starving child.

Jan nudged me awake
to the walls of this new place we call
home. "It's all right," she said
and slept. And I lay awake
the rest of the night, listening
as the wind carried the scraps of sound,
bounced them against the house,
muffled grunts of the abandoned herd
searching us out in the night.

Balaam

1

All the way from Twin Falls
Fred came to help out while Jan had
her surgery and Willa took care of the kid
and I and Fred we chopped wood
played cribbage and fixed up the house
while Jan got well. And then we went to
town to find an axe handle and we found
John and a case of beer and we all went
to John's pigpens to see if that old axe handle
he had was out there

2

There was this man sez Fred
up to Hailey who drove all the way to
Missouri to buy these walking horses
and John sez isatso and Fred sez he paid
a hell of a price and John sez he was in
Missouri once and they raise good hogs there
and Fred sez he bought two mares one stud and a
gelding he didn't know why he bought the gelding
and brought them back to Idaho and John
sez that's too far to haul hogs he wouldn't
do that and the stud, Fred sez, keeps breaking
fence and then goes after the gelding
and finally that man he's had enough
so he ropes the stud and throws him and
castrates him right then and there
by god that stopped that and John sez
boars generally leave barrows alone

you can leave them in the same pen and Fred
sez he never got a colt out of that stud
all that money wasted

3

John sez he had a ewe that kept breaking
fence and Fred sez oncet a animal starts
it's hard to stop and John sez one day he had it
so he got a length of hose and chased her
and Fred sez his brother was good with a black-
snake and used it on bulls and John sez he
caught her and whipped her good till her ears bled
and she jumped back in and Fred's brother
could tick a fly off a horse's ear and that ewe
lambed that night but Al Fred's brother could
lay one open he whipped hell out of that black
English bull one day and John sez somebody
shoulda whipped him because that ewe and her
lamb both died but Al never hit a man with
a whip so John shouldn't ask him he'd have to find
somebody else

4

And I told about Wesley Steven's proud cut
stud back in Texas and John sez he was there
once and he saw a damn big hog farm there
and Fred sez what's proud cut and John sez
whoever cut that horse never got the squealer
and that horse shoots blanks but he keeps
shooting and Fred sez isatso? and John sez yas
he seen a boar that was castrated proud
and he bred any sow that would stand
but she wouldn't pig and Fred sez so that's the
squealer and I sez Wesley Steven's stud

mounted a mare but she wasn't ready and John
sez that's what they'll do they aint got no
sense and they hurry too much and Fred sez
he knew a man oncet that way and he's in
prison and I sez that mare laid back
her ears and kicked that stud's belly open
and John sez that's the good thing about hogs
they don't kick and Fred sez that sonofabitch
got sentenced to forty years and I sez Wesley
had to kill the stud because he was ruptured so
bad and John sez his proud cut boar died
of the blood poison and Fred sez that aint
a long enough sentence for rape they oughta
gut shoot the bastard and I just thought
that poor son of a bitch, that poor sonofabitch

5

That same feller from Hailey
who castrated his stud sez Fred was out
walking and he saw a doe and fawn
and John sez he didn't see even one
goddam deer the whole hunting season and I
sez I didn't even go and Fred sez the
doe jumped the fence but the fawn couldn't
and John sez his big white sow's got to
fence jumping and he can't hold her
in and I sez he oughta get a
electric fence and he sez he'll maybe
ring her nose or chop it with a butcher knife
that'll by god do it and the guy runs up
and grabs the fawn and tries to cut its throat
and John sez even that don't always work so I
say why not? and he sez it'll stop rooting
but not jumping and Fred sez that fawn

stomped the piss out of the guy and put
bruises all over him and got away
and John knew a man that got stepped on
by a circus elephant named Jerry Bush
and it broke his foot and
I sez that hurts (I know I broke my foot and
it hurt like hell) but John sed he never
felt it but he walks with a cane
and that guy fell in a ditch on the way
home and broke his leg and when they found
him he was crawling and he kept saying
where'd that little fucker go?

6

John found the axe handle but it wouldn't
work so we drank beer and I started to tell
about balling a collie dog when I was fourteen
but didn't. Besides it wasn't me it was Kenneth
Bullard and it wasn't a dog but a cow and
he stood on a box and she shit his pants full
down around his ankles but I wasn't even
there I just heard and John talked about farming
and Fred talked about Idaho and I got drunk
and went off by myself and didn't say anything but just
kept thinking about all them hogs
that used to be mine, all mine.

Epilogue

What might have been and what has been
Point to one end, which is always present.

"BURNT NORTON"

In my beginning is my end.
...
In my end is my beginning.

"EAST COKER"

T.S. ELIOT

Months begat seasons begat a year
another
begat a child, another
begat all the successes: advancement,
rank, salary equal to almost one-
half the yearly inflation,
begat respectability, political acumen

voted for all the losers,
Ananias Frogeyes elected, reelected, scholarly insight
studied the use of feminine endings in Milton
by the book, rocked no boats
therefore happy *was* Dave, indeed, passive

Jan made it official,
asked: are you happy?
replied: of course. Why not?
asked: are you sure?
replied: I'm very busy. Do you need something?

And on Saturday Jan left
for groceries, I baby-sat

studied scientific humanism, read essays
she returned, honked
honked, honked
until outside came Dave, passive
said get this sonbitch unloaded
replied: I beg your pardon
said either get it unloaded
or go back and set on your butt

I'll do it

Saw in the pickup bed
fence wire, twenty cedar posts, sheet iron,
one dozen 2 × 6 boards, a gunnysack
behold, a gunnysack, *tow sack*
tied with a strand of wire
baliwore I've seen that before
a voice whispered, where have you been,
Jan? Jan where have you...
tow sack while I watched
      moved

And I *known*
I known whatall's in that towsack's
trouble, break any fence
any man can build or fix
lay in mud, dig holes
belly up to the sun, eat
anything can be eat, gnaw
whatall'll hold still to be gnawed
piss me off worse'n anything alive
bring out all the worse
all the best
   in me

behind the spare tire another sack
behold squirmed
tow sack moved, rolled, tow sack
squealed, squirmed, rooted, tow sack
tied with baliwore grunted
but it caint holt it long
don't worry about being polite
you got to hurry
it'll get out goddam
                  another one

Day's Work

Morning

Hello?
Hey, Dave?
John? What time is it?
Did I wake you up, Dave?
No. I had to get up and answer
the phone. John?
Dave, you sed you'd come hep me
if I needed some one day and I do
come on over.
What time is it, John?
Put on your tennis shoes and
run that mile you do
I'll have breakfast ready
in a half hour when you get here
we'll fix dinner and supper too
leave Jan a note
it isn't no use to wake her up
tell her you'll be home
this afternoon or evening
it's some things I gotta get done.
John?
I'll see you in a few minutes
we'll eat and get started.
     John?
Bye.
       John? It's
five o'clock in the morning.
         John?

After an All-Night Farrow

The thin moon
burns silver
in henlight.

Then gold lace
falls like dew
on the sheet-iron roof.

Now sun sprays
the pasture
and the duroc boar's shoulders
with fire.

Rooster: flap your wings!
Scratch up
a breakfast song
for these eight
newborn children.

Sonnet on the Sun, Rising

Cold. Last night a skiff
of snow. So I
got up five o'clock, made
a fire. Watched the sky
                        unbuild.
I mean, I'm
drinking coffee
                by myself. Shivering.
And I'm cold.
    So it's time, you
    wonderful son
of a bitch. Get on up.
                    I'm ready.
                        Now.

Phone Call

Hello.

Hello, Mr. Williamson? This is David Lee, I live in Paragonah.
During my morning run I passed by your stockpens west of
Paragonah and I saw that one of your cows, the black white-face, I
think, seems to have calved during the night. I think around sunrise,
the calf was still steaming, at least I think so. But the cow seems to
be in some trouble, I think her uterus has prolapsed and she
probably needs some help. I was running and I didn't stop and walk
over to see, instead I turned around and came back to call and let
you know so you can go out and see if she needs help.

Who's this? Is this church business?

No, no. Wallace, I'm the guy who runs out by your stockpens every
morning. You wave at me. Today I ran early and saw that you've got a
cow in trouble. She's an Angus-Hereford cross. She's calved and her
vagina has protruded. You ought to go out and check on her as soon
as you can.

Is this about selling Amway?

Listen:
goddammit, this morning
in your west pen
the black balley dropped her calf
and her ass is out
down to her knees.
She needs help.

Oh goddam
it's that two-year-old heifer

I didn't know she was that close
I gotta go.
Look mister whoever you are
you call back
take and give my wife your name
I owe you
but I caint talk now
I gotta go
but I sure thank you
I'll make it up to you
someday somehow
                    Bye

January: Unloading Feed

Godamitey it's cold
that damn wind don't help a thing
I think I may be loosing
another finger and two toes
and that aint the coldest part

I heard spit freezes
about fifty below
so hold it in I don't want no holes
in the side of the barn
when it's that cold
pee stacks up
my daddy sed oncet
he's in Montana with a womern
had to chop her loost
from the ground

hurry up and get that other sack
out the truck
let's go in and warm up
before the rest of us freezes
and falls off

Fence Repair

What's the matter with you today
sed John you and Jan fighting?
Oh no I said it's not that
it's a letter I got that's bothering me.
Must be from the govament
or the insurance, I can understand that.
No, John, it's not them this time
it's from a friend.
Did he die or summin?
You aint sed a decent word all morning
I might as well be working by myself
and let you set on the nailkeg
unrolling barbwore

Oh dammit, John,
it's just a letter that pissed me off,
I said. It's from a writer who saw something I wrote
about coyotes killing sheep
and he wrote saying that never happens.
He sez what? sez John.
He said there's no documented evidence
that a coyote ever killed a sheep
unless it was rabid, I said.
And he said my story was a lie
and should never have been written.
He's a writer? sez John.
What does he write about?
Oh, he writes novels, I said.
Books about cowboys and Indians
and the California mountains.

He sez that sed John
did he? You know
most chickens I known of
is layers and most folks
I known is liars
and most of them don't know the different
but that don't get in the way
of their opinions.
It was a preacher
got his first call
to come to our town back home
his first sermon that everbody
showed up to hear
was how all people is good
it aint no such of a thing
as a bad person

he wasn't in town half a year
before Travis Newberry
knocked up his daughter in the eighth grade
and he was twenty-four by then.
He'd started preaching late
after giving up on farming
and owning a grocery store
must of been too late
he run out of words after bout a year
we had to elect him to office
to give him something to do.
First thing he voted no taxes
and no pay raises to schoolteachers
so they all known he'd be a good one
mebbe governor some day
had to move him out
of the parsonage and into a house

where he had to pay rent
like real people
so they found him a place
out on the end of town
where they could be alone
with that pregnant girl
they took out of school.
It was skunks out there
a mama and four babies
and his wife and that girl
sez oh they're purdy
let them alone we like them
so he did
by the time she had her baby
they'd killed all their chickens
the Easter ducks and the cats
it was mice and skunks
running all over that place
they couldn't live there no more
so he run for state office

they sent that girl
off to Christian school
we never heard of her again
and tried to raise the baby boy
but couldn't do that neither.
He got elected
on the campaign of no taxes
and close down the schools
cause he blamed it all
on Travis Newberry hanging around
the jr-high parking lot
and moved to the state capital
to live and before

they could rent that house again
they had to set out traps
for two months and rat poison
sed they got twenty-four skunks
but nobody counted the mice
it was awful
took a year for the smells
to go off and it wasn't no hippies
back then to rent it to
they had to wait it out

so he run for Warshington office
six years later
and put the boy in the orphanage
up for adoption
he might of been a scandal
but he didn't get elected
they made him a judge instead
after that and he's rich
still there and being so famous
he don't pay no rent
the state give him a house
and a car and a maid

but that still don't mean he known one damn thing
about people or skunks or mice
or preaching or farming or
running a grocery store.
I seen it with my own eyes
a coyote running through
a herd of sheep and killed nine lambs
just to do it
and we set up five nights
in our pickups waiting for him

until he come back
and he killed four more
before we shot him
and that's nothing to what
Allen Dalley out to Summit lost
that one year when they say
coyotes got half his lamb crop
that's just a bunch of bullshit
because he done one thing
don't mean he knows nothing
about anothern
and if he doesn't know
what he's talking about
you tell him to just keep his mouth closed
or run for office
that's what it's there for
so why don't you forget about it
and you can forget him too for now
let's get to work
cause all this is real
not something in a book
and has to be got done for sure
not just by thinking about it
and if you don't get that frown put in a drawer
this is gone be a long day of work

Faith Tittle

HEBREWS 11:1–3

John, I said, have you
ever spayed a gilt?
What'd you say? sez John
I said castrated a female pig
it's called spaying.
I known that
I known what spading is
I just caint figger out
why you asking

It was this Ag teacher
back home I remember
who wanted to be a vet sed John
he didn't make it neither
so he did the next best
he liked to try
all them fancy operations
he's good on ruptures
and worms and even
untwisted a horse's gut oncet
I heard and cow's eyes
he castarated a bunch of chickens
made them capers he sez
sed they'd grown fancy feathers
and get fat and sell
for a lot of money
but they all died first
and he cut some girlpigs
spaded them up

most of them died too
nobody known if it was his fault
the ones that lived
was just like barrows
ate and got fat and never come in

It was this one womern
in town we called Faith Tittle
back then cause it was her name
call her Judy now I heard
that was real fat
she couldn't lose no weight
if she tried so she taken and went
to the doctor and he give her
thyroid pills and diets
and examinations
finally he sez she has to have
a hystericalectomy for wormen
they gone take all her female parts out
and then mebbe she wouldn't be so fat
doctor told her, Faith Tittle
it's something inside I caint see
some substance I just hope
I can get rid of for you
and then you'll be better off

Faith Tittle wasn't sure
she'd do that cause that doctor
he'd been a Babtist
medical missionary, he played
piano music in his office
and she's a Cambellite
she couldn't trust him for sure
so she went down to anothern

to see what he thought
and he played band music
in his office and was a Methodist
so when he sed yas
she ought to have it all took out
she wasn't married anyway
and was arredy over thirty
wasn't doing her no good
she figgered he'd believe anything
and probley change his mind
about it at the same time
so she sed she wanted to go off
by herself and work it out
where it wasn't no music
playing because that one doctor
he sed we better take out
the whole works and she's afraid
without that she's about as good
as dead and was it worth it

She went to her kinfolk
Leonard Tittle he's a Cambellite preacher
I don't know what kin he was
he'd been a algebrar teacher
at a high school but his breath
was too bad the kids couldn't stand it
when he leant over to help
with their homework
they'd of rather failt than had him help
so he had to finally find
something else to do
that he could be good at mebbe
so he took to preaching
at the Lorenzo ChurchofChrist

she sed she didn't know what to do
he told her some Methodists
and Babtists wasn't all bad
they might not go to heaven
but they could do operations
on earth okay and he'd pray
it'd probley work out

so she done it
they cut her open
both doctors was there at the same time
hauled off a wheelbarrow load
of stuff come out of her they sed
that operation wasn't no more
than sewed back up
news was all over town
from the nurses and doctors and wifes
they found knots of flesh
and hair and a set of teeth
inside her womb growing there
they didn't know how long
and lumps the size of a cantalope
down to a golfball
took it all out and thrown it
in the trashcan
except the hair and teeth they sed
it got put in a jar and sent off
to Warshington to see what it was

She's ruint
all over town they's talking about it
her business was everbody's
and down in the flats
they's ascairt to death of her

say her name out loud
their eyes swelt up like a coffeecup
they sez she been with the devil
you could pull out a wad of doghair
they'd have a spasm
thinking it might be her hairball
I'd of love to had a set
of falseteeth back then
but I never
Faith Tittle had to leave
it wasn't nothing there
for her no more
she went before the Cambellite church
and asked to be prayed for
with the rest of the sick and afflicted
then she changed her name to Judy
they sed and left
dunno whar she went
it don't matter. Leonard Tittle
stood up the churchhouse
sed all things wake to the good
for those which love the Lord
and he's her kinfolk
so I spoze she come out okay
wherever she went
to start over again

but no
I never done one, have you?
What? I said.
Spaded no girlpig
what are you talking about?
I just caint see no advantage
if the boar stays in his pen

where he's posta be
until it's time to turn him in
they eat the same as any hog
either way just the same
so what's the different
why take a chancet
if you aint sure
what you're doing

Building Pigpens

meanest man ever
was Ellis Britton
I known of him for years
before I known who he was
I went to school with his boy Melvin
we called Swamprat
he's half cross-eyed couldn't help it
got killed in the war jumping out airplanes in Francet
he flown all over the world in the army
before he got killed they sed
is it a longboard over there anywheres?
we can put a longboard on the bottom rail
to stop digging out mebbe
so oncet he was driving along in his car
he seen this man building a pigpen
he's doing the front fence
and it was this level he was using
to get it straight because
it was beside his house
you could see it from the road
and he wanted it to look nice he sez
Ellis Britton he stopped his car
rolt down his winder
and sez what in hell are you doing?
you don't use no goddam level to build
no pigpen you stop that
that man he waved Ellis Britton drove off
that night taken and come back
he torn that pigpen apart
right to the ground with a crowbar
sez he couldn't stand it no more

to put on no airs that way
hand me them nails in the sack
them sixteen pennys

he raised hogs for awhile
couldn't stay in the business
he killed his boar one day
this sow was posta be in
he put the boar to her but she
wasn't ready that boar he
didn't want to wait round
got excited cut her side open
with his tuskies
god it made Ellis Britton mad
he run in his house got his gun
come back he shot that boar
in the head but it was a twenty-two
the boar was old had a thick bone
it never killed him at first
he run off squolling
Ellis Britton he chased him down
shot up a whole shirtpocket
full of bullets killing that boar
cut this board off where I marked it
with the nail right there see?
he killed two other pigs
and shot four more other ones
that never died
when the boar went down
he busted the twenty-two acrost his head
and he'd give it to his boy
for a Christmas present
it wasn't even his

he was deer hunting this time
and it was this horse
he'd borrowed from his wife's brother
so he shot this deer
tried to load it on the horse
they's a long ways out
that horse didn't want to carry that deer
he hadn't done that before
so Ellis Britton tried to load him
but he shied
goddam you cut the wrong mark
I sed the one I marked with the nail
where's that board?
you done ruint it find me anothern
so he give it three tries
then he got his gun
shot that horse and walked home
his wife had to call her brother
and tell him so he could go get
his saddle off the dead horse
if he wanted it
how about that one over there
the long one, will it work?

had to put him in jail oncet
it was this boy rode his motorsickle
at night Ellis Britton he was sleeping
rode it by his house on the road
out front riding round these blocks
he went by a few times
woken Ellis Britton up he couldn't
go back to sleep so he got up
went out in his shed and got his rope
he tied it to these two trees

where it went acrost the road so
here come this boy
it's not long enough
is it one any longer out there?
look in that pile over there
he hit that rope right on his shoulders
busted out both collarbones
they sez if it'd been a inch higher
it'd of tore his head off
and broke his neck
soon as he hit Ellis Britton run out
in the street he taken out his knife
and cut holes in both motorsickle tores
he went back in his house
never even called the ambulance
neighbors had to when they heard that boy
screaming Ellis Britton went to bed
bring that one over here
I think it'll be long enough
they arrested him and put him in jail
so next morning
Charley Baker's daughter she was a idiot
her tongue stuck out her mouth all day
slobbered down the front her dress
she brought these breakfast
it was scrambled eggs with applesauce
on top of it she'd fixed
and slud it in his cell
she set down to watch him eat it
like she always did
you couldn't stand to eat with her
setting there slobbering at you
so most prisoners they'd just slud it back
she'd eat it right in front of them

with her fingers
it was puke all over that jailhouse
after breakfast some days
she could remember and find the ketchup
can you cut this one right?
follow the mark right there
don't cut it half in two this time
Ellis Britton he set right down in front of her
on the other side the bars
eat the whole thing with his hands
her setting there watching
when he's done he used his fingers
sopped up the rest
he slud the plate back so she picked it up
and looked at it then she
turnt it up and licked this one spot
Ellis Britton he jumped up
reached his arm through the bars
grapt that plate he sez
goddam is it some more on there?
that's mine you caint have it
Charley Baker's daughter she hollered
like hell and run off
wouldn't bring him nothing else
they let him go that same afternoon
they arrested him and put him in jail

so he got this job as a conductor
and ticket taker on the railroad
he damn near ruint that whole run
it was to whar it was a line
ever Thursday and Saturday
to take the Greyhound bus
nobody would ride the train

see I knew you could do it
if you'd pay attention
that education has to be
worth something you'd think
they sez some folks would go on
to the next town twelve mile away
and ride the bus back or hitch
just so they wouldn't have to have
Ellis Britton help them get off the train
and find their suitcase
he was so mean
how come you just standing there?
find anothern board
we here to work
not just set round wasting time
so then it was this other time he taken and

Coyote Dope

You can make this bait
I heard about from somewheres
all this meat and blood rotted
in a jar that stinks
they can smell and come
if they in the mood for it

is that water boiling?
put them sagebrushes in it
we'll boil the oil off the traps
get the smell gone
when you lift it out the pot
don't touch it with your hands
use them pliers and a hook

I don't use no bait
they too smart for it
somebody turnt a jar over of it
in my pickup oncet
you caint get that smell away
I had to trade it off finally
put the trap under a bush where
they done been before
and sprinkle coyote piss on it

that's purdy hard to get
cept in a magazine
that costs a lot of money
so dog piss or turds work too
piss is better
on the bushes where they smell it
come up and cockt their leg

to piss on top of it
saying they live here now
they get its leg in the trap
that's how you catch them

it can be embarrassing
getting dog piss
if people come up and see
you getting it
have to foller the dog
around with a coffeecup
for a couple of days
to catch enough to work
he don't do it on demand

okay it's boiling
get it out and put it
in the tow sack
we'll get that sonofabitch

The Tree

Ho Dave, John yelled
let's go buy us some pigs on partners
make some money
with this 400 dollars I got.
What, John? I said
where'd you get 400 dollars
did you kill somebody or did
LaVerne win the Publisher's
Clearing House Sweepstakes finally?
Do you want to get some pigs
or not? sed John and I said
John I don't have any money
I can't buy any pigs right now.
Okay I'll loan you half
on not too much innarest
and you can pay me back
we'll split feed costs sed John
come on let's go

Where did you get 400 dollars? I said again
If it's any of your business
I sued myself and won sed John
I said what?
John sez that's a fact
and here's the money to prove it
he put his hand in his pocket
when he pulled it out
all I saw was green wings
fluttering in the afternoon

It was on account of a aspen tree
John sed and I didn't say anything

we was up on the mountain
getting wood when me and LaVerne
seen this big dead aspen tree
standing so I sed
I'm getting that one
LaVerne sez no you're not
it's against the law to cut down
a standing tree alive or dead
I told her that tree couldn't read
it wouldn't know no better
I drove up beside it and got out my saw

I cut a wedge that would of choked
a dinosaur out of it on the down side
and the wind was blowing north
where I wanted it to fall
I taken and cut downwards
on the up side just right
that tree was gone fall
whar I wanted it to
I'd chop it up and load it
I had the truck up close ready
the radio on so I could listen
to the hogmarket on the 12:30 news
it all looked about perfect to me
I finished the cut and
that goddam big sonofabitch
fell exactly backwards
against the wind
I see it leaning toward my truck
I yelled no goddammit the other way
not that way
it wasn't listening
that tree fell right on down

acrost the hood of my truck
busted my windshield out
and a side winder, mashed the cab
buckled the hood up almost in two
knocked the battrey off its ledge
whar it's dangling in the motor well
and bent the radio antenna
where it wouldn't work
I still don't know how much pigs went for
in Omaha, Nebraska on that day
LaVerne stood there and sez
oh no, oh no, oh no

What did you do, then, John? I said
Wasn't nothing I could do
I'd done watched all that was gone
happen, now I had to go to work
show was over and the radio
wouldn't play no more
not even music so I cut up the tree
and loaded it in the back
I figgered it was mine by now for sure
I earned it so then
I had to get the battery
wored back up whar it would hold
and I went to see if it'd crunk
it did and the radiator wasn't ruint
I told LaVerne get in
we started driving home

I wasn't back on the blacktop
more than two miles here comes this law
with his red light flashing
I sed uh oh and LaVerne sez

you better think of something fast
you gone get a big ticket
they'll take your chainsaw away too
I sez like hell they will
I's ascairt I pulled over
that law got out his car
walked to my pickup and leant on it
sez pardon me mister
but did you know your winder
was bursted out? I wanted to say
did you have to go to college
to learn to be a officer of law or
did you come by it natural?
he'd arredy sed bursted
I known he's educated
so I sed yassir I do
and I want to file charges on it

He sez what? LaVerne sez what?
I sez yassir it was this way
I was driving along
minding my own buiness
on this public road
on a Sunday it was this man
drove by me with a load of hogs
in his truck, passed me and
slowed down right in front of me
made me hit my brakes
or I'd of run into him
that law sez both of you
hit the windshield and bursted it out?
I sez nosir that aint how it was
we's right up behind him
one of them hogs in his truck squolt

when he seen us and he taken
climbt up them stockracks
jumped out that truck
right on my hood smashed through
my windshield into the front seat
busted out the side winder
getting out it like to of
ascairt us to death for sure

that law stood up straight he sez
was it a man in a red-and-white
pickup? I sed yas, a Ford
I think he sez with stockracks
sort of like yours? yas
sort of I sed, he sed they open different
I think but they're orange like yours
I sed yas I think that's a fact
he sez did you happen to notice
if one side of his truck was dented up any?
I sed oh yas it looked like itus
mashed in on the off side
like somebody'd backed up on him
at a livestock auction at the loading chute
or something, I's hoping he wouldn't
walk around my truck
to the other side he sed
did you happen to see his license number?

LaVerne had her brains
plugged in that day not me
I wouldn't of known what to say then
she sed officer I seen the first part
it was a ABJ license plate for sure
oh it was so awful I caint believe it

she taken and put her face down
in her lap like she's crying
that law was shook up he sez
she okay? I sed
I was on my way to the hospital
right now I just caint be too sure
he sez you foller me
I'll give you the police escort
he jumped in his car
turnt on his red light and siren
pult out and led us to town and
to the hospital

We had to go in the emergency room
and wait, he come with us
sed can I ast a few more questions?
LaVerne sez oh officer we in shock
I don't see how we can talk now
it's all so terrible and awful
he sed yasma'am I can see that
and don't you worry
I known who the man who done this
to you is and I'm gone get him
for you, don't you think about it any
we gone make him pay a fine
can you just gimme your name
and address? I couldn't think
that tree might as well of
mashed my head in it wouldn't work
the only name I could think of
to given him was Richard R. Nixton
and if he'd of ast for my driver's license
I was dead right there
but LaVerne sez LaVerne Sims

before I could say a word
Box 162 and that was her daughter
Peggy's and Warren's box number
and that law sez how you spell that
I sed L-A-V-E-R-N-E and he wrote
it down in his book but it come out
L period Verne and he wrote the rest
I never sed a word
he sez I'm gone take care of this
for you personally I can promise
you that and he left

We set there for a hour waiting
and two doctors come up to help us
we sed we's just company
visiting a emergency case
that was arredy there
we didn't want to leave
in case that law would come back
see us and track us down
finally he didn't and we went home

About a week later here comes
a official letter from the law sed
dear John Simms we have a eyewitness
account of how you was irresponsible
with your hogs and one jumped out
and bursted L. Verne Sims's winder
at Box 162 of Cedar City, Utah
caused personal and property damage
resulting in bodily injury
and you're liable if you
don't get your insurance company
to pay for this we gone arrest you

with a bench warrant
signed Steve Johnson, officer of the law

I said what did you do then, John
and John sed
I taken and sent that letter
to my insurance sez I didn't know
one damn thing about any of this
I didn't know what to do
they sed they's gone sue me
for a million dollars if I didn't
do summin so what am I posta do now?
three days later I got a call
from Pocatello, Idaho the head office
man sez what's this all about?
I sez I dunno your honor
I'm just a farmer I don't know nothing
about the law or the insurance
or the goverment except taxes and driver's license
so he ast me to tell in my own words
my side of the story
I told him *if* a hog jumped out
my pickup what can I do about it
that hog's got a mind of his own
I caint tell him what to do
or who to go live with
and what's somebody doing
follering me that clost anyway
aint there a law about that?
besides who's gone pay me
for my hog that would of been worth
a hundred dollars at least
if he's big enough to bust out
a winder like that

and now he's gone I think
they stoled him and I ought to
get something out of it
but they done eat it
besides my insurance going up
I didn't think it was my fault

insurance man sez whoa now
when I told him I's ready to cancel
I couldn't afford no raise in price
especially after I done lost
my best brood sow in that wreck
he sez way he sees it
it's a act of God
couldn't nobody of stopped it
and he gone offer a 500-dollar
settlement if they won't take it to court
and if L. Verne Sims sez that's okay
then they won't raise my insurance
and do I know this L. Verne Sims
is he any kin of mine?
I sez no I don't know no
L. Verne Sims or other man by that name
he aint no sexual relation of mine
or otherwise so he sed
will that satisfy you? I sed
I don't spoze I'll ever be happy
about losing a pig that way
but I caint have no insurance going up
so if that's the best I can do
it's better'n I'm usually treated
he understood and said he's real sorry
but he'd do what he could

After that Peggy brought us the letter
mailed to her mailbox
from the insurance and we sed
we'd accept the 500 dollars
and let it go at that
wouldn't press no charges and
in a week here the check was
and a sheet of paper
to go down and get a bid to have
the damage fix they'd pay for that too

I taken the truck to Parkland
he sez John I'm gone bump this up
I can iron this out and get you
a used windshield for about 300 dollars
I'm gone bid this for 500
won't nobody know the different
and I'll take and give you
a good deal when you're ready
for a new car later on
I sed that's fine write her up
he bid it 500 dollars
I sent it in
another week I got another
500 dollars so I went down to A-1 Glass
got me a new windshield
for a hundred dollars and
a radio antenna and got my tractor
power takeoff fixed and the feeder
on my bailer and two new tores
and I still got 400 dollars
for us to spend on pigs
for partners

John, I sed, your hood's
not that mashed up, how'd
you get it fixed?

Man at Parkland's he calls me up
sez John brang your truck down today
I got you a pointment
we'll get her fixed up good for you
I sed nothankyou I believe
I can live with it like it is
he sed goddam you it's a law
you got to have that truck fix
I wrote a bid and the insurance
he given you the money for it
he sent me a copy of the letter
now you bring that truck in
like it sez or I'll call the police
I sed you can go fuck yourself
I aint doing one goddam thing
to, for, with, on, or under you
and if you call the law
you tell him about jacking that bid up
it's my word against yours
I can holler at least as loud
as you can he sez
you'll hear from my lawyer about this
I sed that's fine
tell him don't write me
write my lawyer and I give him
your name and hung up

What? I said. So then
sed John I call Peggy and Warren
sez y'all come out this afternoon

to see us and bring the kids
LaVerne wants to see them and
we'll watch TV and talk
they can play outside
so they did and when they come
I told them kids now look
I done spent all week
getting that truck hood over there
bent up like I need it
I'd done took it off and had it
laying on the ground
so y'all stay away from it, hear?
we went in
five minutes later I heard them
jumping on it I waited ten more
minutes and went out the door
them kids took off to the corral
they'd done the job
I called Warren can you help me
a minute? he come out
we lifted it on the truck
they'd stomped it out almost flat
we didn't even have to monkey
the holes to get the screws to fit
it latched first time
I banged out the cab
with a hammer, and it's almost
good as new it'll last
till I trade it in a hundred thousand miles
or so

so are you inarrested or not?
What? I said interested in what?
In buying hogs on partners

I got 400 dollars left to spent
and I sed I'll loan you half
we'll make us some money
so what kind we gone get?
And I said yes, John, I'm interested
How about durocs?
Judaspriest no sed John
you caint build a fencet strong enough
to hold them let's get black listed ones.
But they get rhinitis, John
and don't grow
Well we damnsure aint getting
Chestnut Whites that'll sunburn
all summer and shake their fat off
freezing all winter I want
dark ones or spotted or listed.
How about Yorkshire?
That's okay if it aint white or red.
Well, John, now listen, we...

Feeding

If I didn't love that boar so much
I think I'd kill him.
Why, John? I said. He's not that old.
For his hide, sed John
look at all them spots
you tell me that wouldn't make
no good rug or billfold
hanging on the wall
with the hair on
them spots all sticking out
except I don't know how

How what? I said
Tan that hide soft with the hair on
caint you pay attention?
give him some more
he's still hungry
I seen him holt a whole cantalope
in his mouth at oncet
he can eat more'n that
I think it takes a special juice
or summin I know if you rub the hide
with his brains after you bust
his head open with a axe
the hair'll fall off and the skin go soft
but I caint do it the other way
besides if I go to all that trouble
I'm having scrambled eggs on them
I'll hang the hide on the shed
and buy a billfold
I don't need one that bad anyway

back home Rufus Garner
was the undertaker and he known
the secret of how to do it
he made all his belts and stuff
and his wife name Edna Mae
about the purdiest purse of horsehide
she'd wear on her arm
to the funerals and picture show
she told everybody Rufus could do anything
with a dead body except
make it talk or have supper
he could fix them up no matter
how bad they was busted
or eat up with the disease

oh my god she'd say
you should of seen that one
they turnt him on his face
when they operated and all his blood
run to its head and it swole up
its face turnt blue when it died
we gone have to use the suction
get all that out and it's jelly by now
it'll just set in the sink
till we thru and then
it won't warsh down
I'll have to get it out with a soup dipper
if you had a cup of coffee
in your hand when she talked like that
you'd have to set it down somewheres
you couldn't finish it no more
you'd lost the taste by then
this other one
you should of seen she'd say

it was like you taken a razor
cut it round and round
whar he went thru the windshield
his eyes wide like this
staring at you whar Rufus
couldn't find his eyelids to pull them shut
till he got all the swollen out
and its face to go back down
from the size of a basketball
the cuts pult shut and sealt
but the casket will be open
so help me god you can come see
what it looks like right now
Rufus got tored of all that blood
up his arms he's taking a rest
so come on it aint nobody there

the town idiot beside the Bakers
and Fosters was name Jasper
back then that's what we called him
he'd come in to see the dead bodies
if they wasn't tore all apart too bad
he couldn't take that either
till Rufus was done with them
but he liked to see them on the table
he wouldn't touch them
but only stand and look
so oncet one had his stomach muscles
wad up like they do sometimes
oncet in awhile they'll blow out
like they been holding their breath
or their legs'll move
this time it set up straight
Rufus hadn't sewed its mouth shut

so it hung open too
like it was getting ready to talk
Jasper didn't wait
he turnt round fell
right into the closet
where they kept all the funeral clothes
they put on dead people
got tangled up in hangers
started hollering and jerking
like them episcoleptics do
they had to call the sheriff to help
get him out of there

so Rufus got his start in Wyoming
right after he went to funeral school
in a little town somewheres
he run the undertaking
and a taxidermist shop
with a wall between
but the same working room in the back
behind that was where they lived
and the storage room
they's so poor at first
they didn't have no furniture
to set on like chairs
it was two sawhorses and a used door
for a table to eat off
with all the deerheads he's fixing
on the wall watching them
Edna Mae sed they slept in the caskets
when they went to bed at night
and if it was a big one left over
they could sleep together
when their baby got borned

it was a baby coffin they had
for a crib
for the first two years it was alive
until it got used up
but it never known no better
they had to get by

Rufus sed his best one was there
that he almost couldn't get fix
it was this trapper's wife that died
in the winter in January
too much snow and too cold
to bring her in for the funeral
he laid her out straight in the bed
opened the winder while he left
to run his traplines
she's froze when he got back
he couldn't sleep with her
in that bed and it wasn't nowhere else
to put her in the house
he had to store hides in the attic
so the bears wouldn't smell them
and wake up in their holes
come out after them early
he taken her outside
stood her up in the woodshed
till the weather turnt
whar he could bring her down

so when it did he did
took her to the doctor first
so everybody'd know he didn't kill her
she died of the pneumonia
doctor looked her over to see and

sed so for a fact
then he took her to Rufus
to get her ready

Rufus sed he never seen such
a sight as she was
he didn't know what to do
her face was about two foot long
chin hung down on her chest
both jawbones out of its socket
he thot she's the ugliest womern
he ever seen till they showed him
her picture what she's posta look like
he sed what in the hell happened
how'd her mouth get that far
down under her nose?
that trapper sed I be damn
I never noticed I been with her
so long till right now
she'd been dead about two months

ever day that trapper he'd go out
whar she was in the shed
to cut wood for the fire
he'd have to do it mostly at night
working in the day by hisself
he broke off the nail
in the rafter of the shed he hung
his lantern on so he could see
he didn't have anothern
it wasn't enough light on the floor
so he taken and prized
her mouth open to where
he could hang the bail of that lantern

behind her front teeth
to hold it up and it worked
he could see to chop that way
but they figgered
when he done it ever night
that lantern thawed her out
her mouth'd start to hang open
a little till he'd finished chopping
take it off and she'd freeze back up
after two months
her face looked like a boilt clam
hanging open but it happened
so slow he never noticed it
sed he hadn't paid a whole lot
of attention to her face in years
Rufus had to go to the carpenter's
and borrow a furniture vice
to squeeze her head shut
broke both jawbones doing it
he sed he learnt a lot
and the box was open at the funeral
they sed she just looked dead
not horsefaced

he could tell me how to
do that hide with the hair on
if I wanted to kill that pig
but I don't
I don't have the money to buy
another boar right now
I better keep him
you don't need no rug anyway
if you want a hogrug
why don't you kill one of yours

instead of wanting mine?
Give him some more feed I said
you trying to starve him to death?
he's just trying to get by too

Fat

I wish I had the trick
to get these hogs to grow
sometimes I wonder
if it's something wrong
with this pen or not

this is the slowest growing
bunch of pigs I ever had
they just won't eat

I had this cousin oncet
name Roy Don Staples by marriage
he wasn't no sexual relation
of mine but he could teach
them pigs a thing

he's 200 pounds
when he's ten years old
watching him eat
was a education in appetite
when he grown up
he's a barber

he cut your hair
he'd sweat and grunt
round you
like he's gone die
of heatstroke

he's so fat he had to hold
his arms straight out
to cut hair

couldn't even cocket
his elbows

it was enough lard
on his belly
you could deep-fat fry
a ostrige's neck

when he's fourteen
his mama and daddy
set him up a table
by the pigpens
to show him what he looked like
eating

after the third day
hogs wouldn't come out
of their shed
they so embarrassed

he swallered a avocado seed
choked to death on it
and died when he's twenty-seven back then
took four days
to find eight men willing
to be pallbearers
that casket's so heavy

I even put sugar mash
in their feed
and wormed them twicet
they just won't grow
goddam them

if I didn't have so much money
invested I'd sell them
for shoats and they sed
the ropes busted
at the cemetery

his box fell
in the hole
when they's lowering him
they just covered him up
I wasn't there
let's go

mebbe they'll eat
if we won't stand here looking
Mama used to say
it aint polite to watch
fat folks eat anyway
it makes their self conscious
and some might get
the complex from it

Arthritis

for Ken and Bobbie

Can you come help me a minute?
Take and grab this thing right here,
now put them pliers on it there
and hold, I'll get a clamp on
wait a minute, just hang on
right there, there. Okay
youg'n leggo it's done and I thank you

I caint grab holt of nothing tight
today my arthritises is bad
and I haven't got no grip
I swallered four aspurns for breakfast
but they aint working yet
I wisht I had me a copper bracelet
they say helps out when you got it on
or one of them Mexican chinchilla dogs
you can set with it in your lap
and watch TV and it keeps
the arthritis away

Ruby Patrick back home had one
she's Kay Stokes's daughter
married this Jack Patrick rancher
he hit oil everwhere he stuck a stick
in the ground just like Kay Stokes done
so she's rich on both sides
but she had arthritis anyway
in her fingers and toes I heard
went all over to them specialists doctors
spend a damn backseat full of money

to find out they couldn't do nothing
and then asked old man Cummings
who could take warts off of you
what to do cause he'd know
he sez get you one of them Meskin
dogs without no hair on it that can fit
in a teacup they advertise in *Grit*
and the funny books and set with it
in your lap a hour a day
and it'll be a whole lot better
but it won't never go away
you might as well get a marriage license
to it so she did

I heard she paid a hundred dollars
for that dog and got papers
to prove it was a real one so
when Kay Stokes heard about it
he thrown a fit till his face swole up
like a tomater sez what the hell
goddam good is that thing?
he had half the money in the world
but a hundred dollars for a dog like that
was one too many for him that day
can it hunt? he sez can it swim?
can it bring back a duck or a quail?
that sonofabitch caint even set up
in the front seat of a pickup
and see out the winder
what possessed you to pay good money
for a little shiteater fycet?
she sed you get out of here right now
it's none of your bidness what I do
and it's not one penny out of your pockets

so you don't have nothing to say about it.

Any penny spent in this town he sed
is a penny that could of been mine
but he went and left anyway
he never did like that dog
but that was okay
that dog never had no love
for him either

she'd set on the furniture
in her living room with that dog
on her leg and if anybody come in
it'd commence to growl and shake
all over, its lip would come up
eyes'd bug out like grapes
on a mustang vine
that dog known in its heart
it could whup anything alive
that come in or around its house
or the car if it was in it
you could set there and talk to her
for a hour or shell peas all morning
that dog'd never take its eyes off you
or quit snarling, it didn't like nobody
except her and that included her husband
but she sed it did help her arthritis
and she liked it so there you go

Then these sorry poor people
come to town in a whole carload
it must of been a dozen of them it seemed
we figgered they traveled from one town
to anothern looking for handouts
after they left

nobody got a for sure count
on all them kids
but it didn't seem no way
he could of got the back winders
in his car closed
he'd of had to cut off seven arms
and a leg and three heads

they showed up at the churchhouse
Sunday morning and sed
they want to join up, man sez
he wants to address the congergation
sed my kids aint ate a good meal
in a week now what y'all
gone do about it, brothers and sisters?
Wasn't nothing they could do
except have a prayer and take up
a collection but they didn't get much
so somebody sez I think it was
Billie Hill we could bring them back
some food this evening
at the prayer meeting so they did

Mizrez Patrick she brung twelve quart jars
of homecanned peaches she was proud of
she won the blue ribbon almost ever year
at the far and sez I hope you enjoy them
but could I please have the jars back
when you done? she's polite that time
he sez yasma'am whar do I brang them?
she sez address on the jarlabel
so they loaded it all up in his car
and he taken and drove off
didn't even stay for prayer meeting

next morning here he comes
up the street dragging a kid's wagon
nobody known where he got
probley stoled it with all them jars
in it empty none of them even warshed
and knocks on the door
she sed did you eat all that fruit arredy?
when she seen the wagon
on the sidewalk he sez
good godamiteychrist lady
when we eat fruit we eat fruit, by god.
Neighbors seen her
sed her face and jaw went so tight
she could of bit a hole in a crowbar
never sed nothing
went out the door and picked up three jars
in each hand and went in with them
then come back for the rest
he never offered to help her carry them
but when she come back he sez
anybody in there happen to have a cigarette? she sed
nobody in that house smokes
that I've ever heard of
he sez well that's your bidness
I expect not mine
she sed it certainly is
shut the wooden door when she went in

he set down right by the yard gate
started picking his nose and whistling
like he worked there for them
for a living at their house
waiting, he's a professional
she seen it right then

through the windercurtains
he's gone wait her out till she come
and sed what do you want?
that's how come he had the wagon
to carry more back to where he come from
well he had the wrong lady
just cause she was expensive
lived in a big house
and had a fycet she was still
Kay Stokes's daughter and that dog
had papers to prove who he was
so she let the sun shine on him
all day till the afternoon
she opened the door a crack
he started to get up probley thought
she's gone offer him some lemonade
here come that dog out the door

he sez hey lady your shiteater
he never got to finish
that dog was on him
went around his ankle three times
torn his sock right off his leg
put a swok up the back his shirt
like a lawnmower run over him
lit in his hair
grapt a mouthful out and about dug
a hole in his head with his back feet
in about a second and a half
GODAMITEY SONOFABITCH he yelled
jumped up and tried to run
but the dog got in his eyes
and scratched his face
he put his foot in the wagon

and it took off the other way
he fell down on the fence
ripped his britches hollering like a elephant
with its tail in a knot
got up and run down the street
that dog chased him a block
bit him on the finger when he swatted
at it running never broke a stride
he's gone
they left the wagon right there
on the sidewalk for a week
where he turnt it over
but he never come back for it
nobody saw them again
so they give it to the school finally

she said Carlos!
that's what she called that dog
you come right back here in this house
right now, I didn't say
you could go outside
that dog spun round in the street
and went home like a whirlwind
was after him
went through that front door
right between her legs
and she shut it, it was all over
nobody ever heard what she sed
to that dog or about it
she never mentioned it again

but that dog held her arthritis down
for a many a many year
she'd set with it and pet it

in her lap and even Kay Stokes
sed it cut down on the doctor bills
and the aspurns from Bob Collier drug
but he never did say it was worth it
but then he wouldn't
he wouldn't give a inch for nothing

so I wouldn't mind having one
I'd go watch TV with it
and let you fix this damn bailer
I caint figger out why that feeder
don't work and I caint get this wing nut
unscrewed come help me
don't just stand there looking
I told you my fingers don't work today

Separating Pigs

That one's gone be hard to catch
I can tell you now for a fact
he's one the fastest pigs
I ever seen
we'll have to get him in a corner
there he goes
get that othern, right there

I wisht I could find me a track
and race him
we'd win us some money
but it aint one around here
State Legislature wouldn't let us
race pigs anymore'n bet on horses
if they thought we's enjoying it
we'd still have to catch him first
you caint grab him
if you don't bent over
goddam there he goes
you'll have to move faster than that
we need old man Benson
to give you running lessons

we's cutting wood
up around the deep sinks back home
on top the Sawmill Road
my brother'd take off the back tire
put on a belt and rig up
the sawblade
one day here come old man Benson
before he got killed in the wreck
to see what we're doing

and tell us we not doing it right
that sawblade slips off
and comes right at him
usually he's crippled
caint hardly move
this time he seen it like a deer
run off to the side
right in this pond of water
almost drownded before
we could get to him he's so fast
that sawblade
buried itself in a tree trunk
four steps from where he was
so deep we couldn't get it out
if he hadn't of moved that fast
we'd of took him down
for cordwood and it's still there
unless somebody cut it down
you couldn't pull it out for money
he was so fast that day

okay here he is
let's get him this time
before he gets away again
head him goddammit head him

Morning Coffeebreak

The difference between now and then
is when I's young
all I wanted to do was run off
and find me a river
or a stocktank with a tree by it
to hang my clothes in
so I could cool off and swim

now I just think about that mountain
and an aspen tree with leaves
that won't hold still to see what color it is
even when the wind don't blow
the bark so white it's cool
in the afternoon when I set down
with my back up to it
watching a chipmunk go down a hole
and one of us goes to sleep
and the other one don't care
whether he dreams about him or not

Machinery

Hand me them pliers sed John
or look in the box and see
if it's some vicegrips in there
I can get a holt on this with
I wish to hell I'd never bought
this damn swoker used
it's give me trouble
from the day it's born to me
I caint figger why this damn
feeder bar's stuck this way
but if I can turn this one mebbe
OW goddammit that catch lever
kicked me on the knee
go get a sledgehammer
hit it with it
no don't
get me a monkey wrench
mebbe that's what I need

1

Robert Milton had the worst luck
with farm machinery
of anybody I ever known
from the beginnings
he should of been something else
besides a farmer I think
he hitched a ride on a manure spreader
when he's a kid about fourteen
the driver thrown it in gear
to where the spindle turnt
give me a screwdriver
is it one up there close?

I got to get this one out of here
one of them teeth got him
no not a damn Phillipson head
a real one gimme
the woodenhandle one
whar he's laying down hiding
that spindle spine come up
on his face and torn him open
he lost a eye out of it
never could see out of it again

nope that don't do nothing
that's not it from here
look you climb up and thrown
it in gear and let me see
what it does if it's going in
he never did have any
of his equipment that worked
he'd buy a milking machine
it'd be hook up backwards
splatter milk all over the barn
then when they'd fix it
the bacterias was in the lines
he'd have to tear it all down
and start over
let it off I caint see nothing here
I'll slide to the other side
see if it's something there
so when he put it back
the pump went out
had to get a new one
then his electricity'd have
one of them power surge
blow it again

shock the cows or something
okay put it in one more time
they got to where
some dried up and the others
kicked so much he quit
and went to crops
let it off slow
slow I sed caint you hear?
do it again oncet more
wait a minute stop now
push it in slow and let me
get my head up here
whar I can get a look at it
now do it

2

he had about four or five tractors
in a row none of them any good
he'd have to have two at a time
one to be busted down
grinding the valves or
putting in gaskets or rods throwed
right there you can stop
I think I see something over here
they was all ruint oncet
he had hay had to be cut
so he used a horse-drawn mower
he borrowed from his daddy's place
where it'd been setting out rusted
but the horses wasn't used to it
they hadn't pult it before
only wagons and kids riding
so this pheasant flown up
to whar one reared

the othern went to the side
that mowing machine must of
hit a ditch or a rock
nobody seen it
he sed the last he remembered
was that bird and he
didn't have no shotgun with him

lookie here I be damn
these gears out of whack
they aint mesh up
no wonder it don't turnt
how'm I gonna get them back now
you got any idears?
can you see it? right here
bend down you caint see it
if you don't bent over
get me a pry bar of some kind
is it a heavy screwdriver
or a longhandle wrench?
if I can get this one on

so it thrown him out of the seat
down in front of the cutters
the horses kept going
give me it here
I think that'll work
he got caught in the pointed guards
on the cutter bar
drug him halfway down that field
see there it went on
now how come it's coming off?
something's loost somewheres
scalped him

cut off a ear and a kneecap
three of his toes
slit him open all the way down
one side before it thrown him out
he was a bloody goddam mess
all over the kitchen when he got back home
crawling all the way
look at this support bar
it's cracked clean through
you sonofabitch

3

now how we gone hold that together
I want you to tell me?
this aint no classroom
don't stand there studying
with your hands on your hips
pick up a hammer and hit it
see if that'll work
he's the one you might of read about
the goverment loaned him
money to put in one of them pits
in his cowyard to rake the slurry in
so it wouldn't be muddy
on his shoes in the yard
it'd turn into that
methane gas

We got to get this braced somehow
or it'll come right back on itself
it might throw that whole rotater
off if it does it again
how them cows done it
nobody knows it shouldn't of happened

but they somehow knocked the lid
down into the pit
where it was a open hole
in the corral they couldn't have
so the hired hand
didn't know no better
none of us had saw one of them before
he clumb down in after it
never come out
that gas killed him
before he known it
Robert's boy was there too
he went down after him
it kilt him too that fast
both of them down there dead
you could see them not breathing
his wife called the police
and the sheriff went down
after them with a hankerchief
over his face but it wasn't enough
now there's three of them dead
they had to get a ambulance
and a foretruck there with gasmasks
to get their bodies out
it was in all the newspapers
Life magazine and *Grit* I think
everbody heard about it
it was him and known he shouldn't of
tried it because we all knew
he didn't have no luck
with machinery
it's got to be welted

4

I can spot it here
then run a bead along here
to holt it agin the wall
where it won't wiggle loost
but I have to get it home for that
how am I gone fix it for now?
is it any bailing wore up there?
it was a call one night
I answered it and my brother sed
hello John
I sed hello how are you?
he sed I'm fine but Robert's not
he's dead
look at the seat post
under where I set
I think I wrapped some around there
in case I might need it
brang it here

they sed he died of a heart attackt
about nine a.m. in the morning
and didn't come home for dinner
Irene didn't think
much about it
and then for supper
she got sort of mad
it was bowling night
she went alone
got back home about nine
he wasn't there
yeah that's good
give me both of them
I'll wire it in two places

where'd I put them pliers?
she called the sheriff
it was a new one the othern's dead
to go look and there he was
by his pickup dead too

after they hauled him off
they went to bring the pickup home
couldn't start it
battrey's down
he played the radio a lot working
I figger when it wouldn't crunk
that was one too many for him
he jumped out to kick it
probley killed him
too much for his heart
he'd seen enough

okay put it in
let's see if it's gone work
there it is
I think that'll hold for now
till tonight or when I can
get it home to my welter
don't you walk up
on that side of it when
it's running though
it might not holt
if that bailing wore busts loost
it might slung that whole wheel off
it could kill you
and bust your leg

that's good enough for now
let's go to work
and get this hay cut
before something else
decides to fall apart and bust

Castrating Pigs

1

All right that's the first half
done and through
you want to take a break
go set in the shade a minute?
John sed and I said yes
my back hurt from bending
while I worked the knife
and needle but
my half was done and I got to hold
the pigs while John cut
and gave the shots

you like doing the cutting
don't you? sed John and
I said no John I don't
I didn't say and you know it
but John knows damned well
that I don't like castrating
that it makes me almost
as nervous as pig killing
you want a coldbeer? he sed
I said no John, not till we're through
he sed it won't give you
the shakes just one
I said I'm through cutting
it's your turn anyway
John sed if that's how you want it
I said John that's what we agreed
I'd cut half and you cut half
I've done almost a hundred pigs

it's your turn
but only half of them was boy pigs
John sed and I said yes John
but I earmarked the gilts too
and John sed yeah but
you're better at that than I am
and I said no I'm not John
you taught me how to do that
John sed that's how come
I'm a good teacher
and I knew John was
going to try to get me
to cut the rest of his pigs

2

You got any hangnail clippers?
sed John I got one
it's driving me about crazy
to where I don't think
I could hold on to a pencil
or a knife much lest
one of them shot needles
it's so aggervating
aint it funny how something
that little can stick out
and hurt so much
whar you caint even concentrate

Chant Lee back home
that run the flower shop
him and John Heller was moving
this stove out of a widow's house
cause she bought a new one
on a Monkey Ward sale catalog

but if they'd put the new one in
for her she could save more
that's what she told the preacher
he calt them on the phone
to do their Christian duty
so when they was wallering it
away from the wall
to unhook it Chant Lee
got it sideways so the ovendoor
come open and then it
tipped upside the frigerator
slamt back shut
he started hollering stand it up
stand it straight up
John Heller set his side down
where the stove was even
but Chant Lee was caught
in the corner he yelled
open the door open the ovendoor
John looked down
it was shut on his pecker
caught in the side
he couldn't even jump
up and down it might of tore off
so he opened it so
it come out but Chant Lee
sed he had to go to the bathroom
see if it was ruptured
or bruised up too bad

he come back in a minute
John Heller was almost bawling
he sed did the stove fall on you
are you hurt? he sed no

Chant Lee sez what you
looking that way then?
he sed all my life I been
about a half inch too short
for anything I wanted to do
I'd give four years off the rest
if I had a pecker long enuf
to get slamt shut in a stovedoor
that's what's the matter
with me so how come
you didn't tell me
you didn't want to cut them pigs?
I thought you wanted to help
when I called you this morning
if you didn't want to help me
you should of sed so
in the first place
I could of got LaVerne or somebody
to come give me a hand
haven't you got no clippers?

3

Last time we done this
my arthritis was so bad
I couldn't hardly hold on
to the tools you remember
I taken and given myself a shot
of that combiotic two times
that day cause my hands
wouldn't work right
my grip was all give out
John I said you did that
when we were cutting that boar
he knocked you down once

and the needle stuck you
and the other time
you sat down on it
where you laid it on the bucket
oh bullshit sed John I never
my hands wouldn't work
and I couldn't put that needle in
whar I wanted it to go
so you gave yourself a shot
in the butt instead I said
no he sed that was a accident
but it wouldn't of happened
if my arthritises hadn't been bad

accidents like that happen
when your hands won't do
what you tell them to
it was this man name Bill Wilkins
I known back then
who was a countant and did taxes
for the expensive people
who needed it so they
wouldn't have to pay the goverment
he had arthritis
almost as bad as mine's acting today
it was a tradgedy
he was showing his wife
this recipe for cooking hotpeppers
he'd learnt from a Mexican
but you had to peel them
so they was doing it drinking beer
it went thru him he had to lose it
went back to the bathroom
was gone a few minutes

she heard this awful hollering
run back there
he's laying on the floor
his britches down to his knees
hollering holding a towel
on his private self
because of his terrible arthritis
in his hands he couldn't
turn on the water faucet to warsh
he'd unzipped and grapt hisself
with all that hotpepper juice
all over his hands
it come off and scalded him
he was in a awful pain
nobody known what to do
he sed he was about to get
them water blisters all over
it was burnt so bad
she called the hospital
to see what to do
they never heard of it before
given her the number
at the capital for the poison control
whar they sed you better
get some butter or crisco grease on it
real fast to get the heat out
it worked he's afraid
they was gone have to operate
but they didn't

he didn't want them to find out
and put it in the newspaper
but they must not of heard
he sed it took three quarts

of olive oil to put out the fire
they never did finish cooking
them hotpeppers after that
he sed he lost the taste for them
all because of his arthritis
and I don't think I've got
no aspurn in my truck for mine
this one hand's purdy stiff
I'll have to hold the knife with
you know I didn't get a cold
that whole winter I give myself
them shots of hog medicine
it's got penicillin in it they say
it works

4

John I said are we going
to finish those pigs today or not?
we've got half left to go
yas we gone finish them up today
I haven't got time
to take two days on it
I'll get it done somehow
even if I have to find a way
to keep from hurting my back
benting over that long
with my bursitis
let's look around see if it's a bucket
I can turn over and set on
to do it so I won't hurt myself
because when we keep on like I was
holding them for you to cut
my back's straight
I can do that all day long
it's that benting over hurts me

got to watch it setting down
even then at my age
something can go wrong
if it's not a natural position
Gideon Clark was splitting rings
they cut off one of them popular trees
that the wood's tough on
and hard to split so they brung it
to him and give it for nothing
to burn but he had to split it
he's old too like me
mebbe a little bit older I spoze
so he set down on the round
he'd drive a wedge in
with a four-pound hammer
turnt around on it and put
anothern in the other side
most times two wedges
would pop it apart or get it
so he could whop it
with a maul oncet and bust it

this one time he's setting there
hammering this green piece
he hit the wedge and somehow
it went down but then
popped right back up and out
that popular wood snapped together
closed right up on his privates
that was hanging partly down
in the split part
like a vice slamt shut on him

oh my god oh my god below me
he bellered loud as he could

tried to stand
tried to roll tried
to pull hisself out
his family heard him in the house
come out to see what it was
but it was too horrible to look
what do we do? his grandboy sez
who was there being baby-sit that day
oh my lord I don't know
his grandma sed I never saw
something like this before ever
Ellis Britton lived two doors down
heard him hollering
come down to see what it was
sez go get a axe and cut him off
then he'll be loost
it's a doctor can sew it back on
oh my god below me Gideon yelled

finally that boy seen the wedge
laying on the ground
where it fell when it come out
he got it back in the split
right between Gideon's legs
about two inches away and hit it
with the hammer four times
before he could get it in
far enough for that wood
to come apart so he could get out
he went straight in the house
went to bed and shut the door
wouldn't talk to nobody about it
his wife had to give
that wood to Ellis Britton

he wouldn't split no more of it
Ellis Britton sold it
to the Babtist preacher at half price
he sed so he wouldn't
have to worry about firewood
and could take care
of the sick and afflicted
see if there's a bucket or something
I could use for a chair
to set on if I have to do this
over there behind that shed
so I don't kill myself
or ruin my back for life

5

John I said if you want me to
I'll stand in the pickup bed
and hold them where
they'll be up high and you
won't have to bend over
would that be better?
oh no sed John that's not
the natural way you do it
where'd you learn a trick
like that from anyway
I never heard of that before
I don't want no hogblood in my truck
and what if you fell
you might bust your head open
it could be dangerous
to do it that way
one them hogs might bite you
on the ankle in there
you'd get tangled up in the stockracks

trying to get loost
it'd get infected and I aint got
no insurance if you sued me
we caint do it like that

we have to do it
the way it's always been done
you know better'n that
you try to change a good thing
never know what might happen
my brother he castarated cats
for people back home
to keep from having too many
running all over town
he'd put them in a army boot
like them you're wearing
upside down and lace them shut
where their butt was up
and he could get them worked on
they couldn't get away
or scratch at him

but this one time he was
coming home from work
they seen him and brung a cat
for him to castarate
he's wearing shoes not boots
it was summertime and too hot
so he couldn't do it
like he always did
he taken off his overalls
he's wearing britches under them
working hay so two layers of clothes
kept him from scratching up his legs

and tied a knot in them
where he could put that cat in
all wrapped up in it and
set down straddled on him

when he starting cutting
that cat had a conniption
to get loost of him
he got one out and was about
to start on the othern
that cat finally bit thru
the overalls his britches was thin
on the butt a old pair
he had on for work
that cat chewed him
right on his intersection and
would of held on
he jumped up sed GREAT godamitey
that cat come out
them overalls like he was shot
out a cannonball
they never did catch him
to finish the job
my brother sed never again
would he ever go to work
without his boots on after that
he pulled his britches down
right there to see
if that cat torn his balls open
it's some things you have to
do the right way or not at all
it can be dangerous

6

John I said do you want me
to cut the rest of those pigs for you?
Do I what? John sed
I said, I said...
look John sed if you want
to cut them pigs well I won't
stand in your way from it
all I want to know is
why didn't you say so
before I almost got started
I don't mind doing everything
your way all the time
but you at least
ought to let me known how it is we're gone do it
so I can make plans on it
we got to work together
if we gone get it done don't you think
but if that's what you want
let's get to it
we're wasting time standing here
you can talk about it later
let's get this work done now
while it's still some light
to see by

Edna Mae

Rufus was the town undertaker
and Edna Mae his wife
lived with him in the back
of the funeral home
where they had another door
it opened to Huffman furniture
he run that too
when it wasn't nobody dead to bury.

You could tell when somebody died
in town, here'd come Edna Mae
down the street wearing her gold
high-heeled shoes
she always wore to funerals
and her mink stole rain or sun
cold or hot she wore it
we all called it her evening gown
the whole town would know
somebody's dead before we known
who it was when we seen
Edna Mae's gold high heels.

She helped Rufus out
with the funerals and dead bodies
putting on their clothes
pinning on the corsages and
getting them right
her and Rufus was artists they sed
and I spoze so
didn't matter how mashed up
they was them two could get them natural
so they just looked dead

and the coffin lid could be opened
at the churchhouse to see
even Edgar Turner and his head
was half shot off.

You'd go to the cemetery
after the funeral and at the end
of the line was Edna Mae
and the preacher and Rufus
to shake hands and help feel sorry to
all the family and watchers
she's as official as the sheriff

so she died of the cancer finally
everybody wondered how
Rufus'd do it to her and then
without her and how he'd dress her
but when we got to the funeral
there she was in her box
wearing her mink stole
and the preacher sez she'd done
wrote out all the plans
for her funeral
and the sermon and the prayers
and the singers and the songs
and before we could even wonder
about it they had the first song
and if I live to be a hundred
I'll never forget it
them singing *oh them golden slippers*
at her funeral
and everybody who was there'll swear
to this day when they went by
her box at the end
she's smiling.

Still Life: Lightning Above the North Fields

*Agreement at variance with itself: adjustment
under tension, as of bow and lyre*
HERACLEITUS

Running on the graveled road
joyously. A small rain, like dew,
all afternoon and an owl

lumped in sodden plumage
tangled in the sleep
of Russian olives. Clouds rush,

thick redolence of sage, reverberation.
Road clings to the shoes. Memory:
Max Cannon & his bay

gelding near Beryl Junction
a hundred yards from the tunnel
last year. A field mouse

scuttles under glistening barbed wire
into shadows of lucerne. Smile,
or the imagination of smile

imagining the scrim of dream
split by a phosphorescent glow,
rumble in the great vault

cry and flutter of wet wings,
"not I, not I" so thin reply.

Hired Hand

You need some help
out to your place for anything?
What John? I sed
It's a man come around
looking for work
here and there he don't charge much
name Norman and he's willing
to work for money

you caint get no good help
I hired this one college boy
from over to Monroe name Cloward
to help me put sheetiron
on my barn roof
that didn't work out
I told him look
I'm gone splain this one time
and did what I wanted him to do
but ever time he walked by
that pile of sheetiron
he'd stand there combing his hair
in the reflection of it
trying to look purdy
all I had out there was me
and them ewes
I couldn't take a chance on it
whatall might be on his mind
I had to work and the ewes
was arredy bred up
I let him go that day

Norman aint too smart
but he aint purdy
and don't worry about it
him and a rooster
could stand there and stare
at a line you drawn
in the dirt with your foot
half the morning till you shook him
but if you tell him
what to do and check up on him
he'll get it done
all of us working together
I imagine we can finish it
before wintertime comes
but he can come help out
over to your place too
I suspicion if you need help
but he aint much conversation
he just understands
whichever you tell him to do
you shouldn't ask him
for anything more than that
that's all you're paying him for

Digging Postholes

was teaching his boy Melvin
how to play some baseball
so he stolt this ball bat
off the churchhouse softball team
brung it home
he opened up the garage door
a little bit he put these little gravels
down on the ground inside
had Swamprat stand there
every evening before dark for a week
holding the baseball bat
and the swallers'd come out
they'd see them gravels
flown down to get it
the way they do
so Melvin when they come in
through the door
he'd see them coming in out of the light
he'd swat at them with that bat
learning to hit baseballs
that's deep enough
I done got a cedarpost
youg'n go ahead and dig the next one
Ellis Britton he'd whup his ast
if he didn't hit some
every night you could hear him
hollering boy you
keep your eye on the sonofabitching ball
you swinging like a damn girl
you want me to get you a orningboard?

Melvin he'd bawl
he'd squowl I'm trying goddammit
Daddy them bastards won't holt still
Ellis Britton he'd holler
just clost your mouth boy
here comes anothern get ready
where'd that tamping rod go?
so he'd hit a few they's all squashed up
out in front of the garage
here come the cats

Ellis Britton he knew them cats'd
bring him bad luck
if he let them stay around
so he taken and borrowed this pellet gun
from the preacher's boy
made this one daughter of his
set on the porch with the gun
while he helped Swamprat
learn to hit baseballs
and shoot them cats when she seen it
sneaking up on the garage
to get them dead swallers
it was this one she shot at
ripped him a little bit somewhars
that cat couldn't think of nothing to do
but climb a tree
it wasn't no tree out there
just Ellis Britton
he's hollering how'd I ever
get a piss-ignorant boy
like you? you done missed anothern
I'm running out of patience boy goddammit
that cat clumb right up him

that one'll be a cornerpost
dig it a little bit deeper okay?
so Ellis Britton
like he got his tit in the wringer
bellers godamitey godamitey
get him off get him off me
Melvin he sez is it one coming Daddy
his daughter she commenced
to pumping that pellet gun up
hollering Melvin Melvin
that cat went right up the side of his face
torn whole handfuls of hair out his head
he couldn't grab it fast enuf
just hollers get him off
get him OFF me
his daughter yells Melvin Leon
Melvin Leon pumps that gun
Ellis Britton's wife comes out the housedoor
screams jesus godamitey judastpriest
Swamprat runs out the garagedoor
he sez whar whar? Ellis Britton hollers
get him off get him off me
that cat about torn his ear in two
he grabbed holt and was hanging on
Ellis Britton's wife she hollers
do summin DO summin
Melvin he sez whar is it whar is it?
his daughter hollers on his head see him
on his head she shoots Ellis Britton
in the shoulder with the pellet gun
Melvin yells I seen him holt still
Ellis Britton's wife hollers help your daddy
HELP your daddy Ellis Britton he yells
goddam what was that?

when that pellet hit him in his shoulder
he turns round Melvin
he hit him in the face
with the baseball bat

the cat ran off and hid
when he fell down
got away

it should be a big cedarpost in the pile
see if you can find one for the corner
so his nose was busted
it broken off half his front teeth
he had them all pult out
got him some storeboughten ones
sez it wasn't worth it to fix them
it costed too much
most was rotten anyways
they had to operate on him
to get that pellet out of his shoulder
that cat never did come back

Melvin didn't get picked
for the baseball team that summer
he could hit but he couldn't catch
he had this one eye it was crossed
he couldn't find the ball
up in the air after itus hit
that's a good one bring it over here
they's afraid he'd get his brains knocked out
if it was a flyball hit on his head
they known Ellis Britton
he'd sue the Little League if it did
so they wouldn't let him play no baseball

they couldn't afford it
stick it in and scrape up some dirt
with your foot and I'll get the tamping rod
so then after that he

The Feed Store Salesman

I aint going to Overbury's feed store
no more if I want to buy something
don't matter what it is
I'll say gimme a little sack
of sixteen-penny nails he'll get out
a big sack sez you'll need more'n that
a week later I done got
three flat tores and nails strung all over
the back of my pickup
or seed I'll say I want
200 pounds of alfalfa seed or
eight pounds of red potater sets
or four pound of arsh potatereyes
I come home with the whole
damn back of my truck full
of seed to plant twenty acres of hay
and the front seat running over
of damn rotten taters
probley left over from his garden

Jiggs King held his own
with him oncet I seen
he come in sed I need to buy some rope
he sez how much you need?
oh he sed we gone stake the calf
in the backyard so enuf to go
from him to the fence
mebbe about fifteen feet or twenty
he pulls about fourteen coils
off that spool sez let's make sure
he don't stranglet on the pickets
Jiggs sed wait a minute

till I get that calf moved up
a little closter to the fence
that's more'n I can afford
but I caint think that fast
he would of solt me
that whole spool for my damn calf

Bargains

You ever bought stuff
on a sell and then had to
spent more than it costed
getting it back right
cause it wasn't worth it
trying to save money? sed John
I said yes I have
I bought a hundred pounds
of laundry soap on sale
that we might as well feed
to the pigs for all it's worth
it won't get clothes clean

don't do that sed John
pourn it on the ground
in their mudholes so when
they waller they'll get clean
LaVerne sent me down
to buy her some jarlids for canning
it was some I aint seen before
on a good buy that day I got
so when she put them on
not a one of them sealt
we got seven jars of sourpickles
seven more of applebutter in the frigerator
to use up before it spoilt
he wouldn't give us our money back
sed all merchandise was as is
he give me another good-bye
I got a whole drawer full
of jarlids won't work worth a damn
if you know anybody needs some

back home Homer McCreary
took and bought him
a toilet-paper oil filter
for his car oncet that was gone
save him fifty dollars over
the life of that car
it might have except it thrown
all its rods in six month
gummed up the camshaft
had to rebuilt the whole engine
toilet paper and slime all over
down in there ruint
Ab Holm the mechanic sed
you might as well of pourt sugar
in with the oil as use one of them
and to save more money
he'd even used that one-sided
toilet paper that goes thu
on your fingers when you use it
so we figgered he deserved it
for being that cheap

I worked the hay combines
when I's younger from Oklahoma
all the way up to Dakota
mebbe even Canada on that one place
I never known how far up we was
so when we finished and come back
I hitched to that damn Amarillo
when I was gone hop a train
from Oklahoma where I worked
back home to save the money
I had 300 dollars I'd made with me
outside town it was a bridge

that went over this river
without no water in it
in that part of Texas
that the train'd slow down for
I had everything I owned
except what I's wearing and
the money I'd made in my pocket
in this satchel I had then
that I'd run my belt through
and cinched up so my hands
was free to grab holt of the ladder
when it went by slowed down
with that satchel banging
on my knees when I run
it had to be a slow pace

I grapt that ladder
tried to climb up but that satchel
went under and was
on the other side hung up
on the bridge where if
I let go to keep the satchel
I'd fall off into the dried-up river
without no water in it and
break my neck in the sandbed
about a hundred feet down
or if I kept on hanging on
I known I'd get tired
fall off under the wheels
get mashed up for something's breakfast
that I hadn't even seen
or cut up in nine pieces

so I held on and pult upwards
hard as I could till my belt busted
satchel fell in the river
probaley floated off when it rained
if it ever did but I's free
clumb on top and rode
while I fixed my belt up
best as I could so my pants
wouldn't fall down

I had to switch trains
at Wichita Falls to get anothern
went where I's going
but the train wasn't stopping
I had to get off however I could
or go to Houston or mebbe El Paso
I couldn't speak Spanish
so I got down on the ladder
ready to jump off outside the trainyard
got my feet moving like I was practicing
running before I hit the ground
then I let go running
fast as I could so I wouldn't fall
all over my face but my belt
busted again or come loost
my pants went down and drug me
right into one of them cholla cactus patches
down around my legs and
some prickley pears too
I had cactus thorns from my knees
to my ast to my elbows
and some in my neck
had to stay in the hospital eight days
took ever penny I had

I mopped floors there
the last three days at night to make up
the rest of the bill
a ticket home from Oklahoma
costed fourteen dollars back then
a whole summer with nothing to show
it didn't even leave a scar

they oughta be a law
against selling cheap stuff
that don't work to save money
cause you loose ever time
I bought them damn sparkplugs
and Japan and points they had
out to Overbury's that worked
for about a week and that's all
now my swoker won't start
and I run the battrey down crunking
I got forty acres of hay for Keith Guymon
to knock down I sed before morning
and I got to tune it up and
buy some more new parts
if you'll go get them for me
I done waste more time arredy
today than I'll ever get paid for
so don't buy me no more
cheap things this time
you keep them for yourself
from now on
don't do that to me no more
so if you'll do that then go on
cause I got work to do

Taking a Break

You ever worry about that boy
of yours? sed John about
the kind of kids he's gone run round with?
John I said I worry about my kids
most of the day and all night
and I don't think I'm ready
for you to prime the pump

no I never meant it that way
John sed it aint no use
to go and get a head start on it
I just wondered who
he's gone grow up and be like
I always heard you's gonna be
like what you grown up round
that and what kind of blood
you got in you
it was a boy back home
come out of good people
his daddy run a grocery story
had a good living
that boy took up with Travis Newberry
before long he's riding motorcycles
all the law known him by name
sure enuf they caught him
busting in to the school
stealing lunch money and then
Ben Edwards' hardware store
they known Travis put him up to it
but they couldn't catch him
sent that boy to the reform school
he's never right after that

them Adams boys got a Mexican sheepherder
he can train the best sheepdog
of anybody round here they say
he takes the puppy away from the bitch
before his eyes gets opened up
let him suck on a ewe
tied up to a fence till she adopts him
he grown up thinking he's a sheep
and hates whatall comes after them
but I dunno if I want a dog
that thought it was a sheep
might not even have sense
to lift its leg to piss on a sagebrush
it goes both ways

some people back home
was so poor they eat rabbits
ever night for supper
so long their kids
would run under the porch
and hide ever time they heard
a dog bark
that's what they sed
but I wouldn't worry
about that boy of yours yet
he's still young
you got a couple years
to let it grow on you
where'd you say them steeples was?

Shoveling Rolled Barley

got this job selling trailerhouses
he couldn't do that neither
he'd run off all the customers
when they'd come on the lot
they'd look at this trailerhouse he'd say
you sure you can ford something like that?
mebbe you better go look at them one's
on the other side the lot
they more for people like you
it don't cost so much over there
you think it's enuf grain here
to fill up them other three self-feeders?
it better be I caint buy no more
so he went out this one time
set up this trailerhouse they'd solt
he was posta get it leveled
and this other guy he'd hook up the plumbing
Ellis Britton he didn't make no balance
in the middle he's just trying
to do it with the screwerup thingamajig
up on the tongue on the front
he's benting the trailerhouse frame
it wouldn't level
he'd screw it up and go look
the bubble would go one way
he'd go unscrew it back down and look
the bubble would be on the other end
he done it twice or three times
he got mad he taken his hammer
started beating on the front of the trailerhouse
looked like it'd been shot
with a cannonful of ball bearings

all them little dents
that other guy who was there working
sez ohmygod Ellis Britton
what you doing?
Ellis Britton he sez
it isn't none of your goddam business
he thrown that hammer down
scrut it up again
but the bubble was off the other way
he set back and screamed
like he's a crazy womern
beat his hands up against the trailerhouse
till they was both bleeding like hell
sez goddam you goddam you sonofabitch
that's enuf in that one
let's pull the pickup over to the one
in that pen it's almost empty
he's so mad he went over and got his torch
he lit it and burnt a hole in the end
of the trailerhouse he sez there by god
how'd you like that? so grapt
that screwerup turnt it up some more
bubble went to the other end
he had both ends of that trailerhouse
a foot up above the middle
it was all warped they never could fix it
his face went purple like a balloon
his eyes almost come out of the sockets
he picked up that torch
cut the tongue right off the trailerhouse
he hadn't put in no leveling blocks
up front that whole thing
come down right on the ground
busted all the winders out and the doors

popped open so they never could get them shut
he's so mad he cut that screwerup
in three pieces and thrown it over the fence
that other guy's just standing there
it wasn't nothing he could do but watch
it wasn't even no telephone to call his wife
he never sez nothing
with Ellis Britton holding that cutting torch
so when he's done
he flung the torch down he sez
that's it I quit
I caint take this shit no more
he walked all the way back
to the trailerhouse lot by hisself
when he got there they arredy known
that other guy drove back and told them
what he'd done but he left
before Ellis Britton got there he sez I quit
pay me off right now
they give him his money too
they known what he might do
at night if they didn't
Ellis Britton he could hold up
his end of a grudge pretty good
help me back up to the feeder
don't let me knock it down
it isn't no sense to doing that
it wasn't nothing left for them to do
he'd ruint that trailerhouse for good
they figgered they come out ahead
if he'd just leave and not come back no more

August: Midnight Farrow

How beautifully brown
and deep
the red gilt's eyes
by lightning.

Hauling Hogs

for JoDee
"How long till we get there?"

If I was to be a driver
forty years I'd never get used to it
or like it one bit
I caint back up a trailer
worth a damn and I don't think
I'll ever get over worrying
about having a wreck
with all them hogs back there

that one truck that jackknifed
up on Black Ridge
they sed he was hauling
200 head of fat hogs to California
because of the train strike
it was pigs all over the freeway
about fifty of them dead
or had to be killed
some froze before they could get to them
I heard they only found
and got loaded about a hundred more
the rest run off in the bushes
when it split open barrows and gilts
I drove up there twicet
to see if I could find them

What would you do John I sed
if you found them?
you couldn't catch them
they'd be too wild by now

I'd go home and load up
me a little boar and donate it
to the wild herd if I seen
any of them girlpigs running round
them barrows aint doing them
any good they might as well
run off and live in San Francisco
I'd start a wild herd up there
get me a license to guide
or a brandingiron to catch strays

about ten years ago they say
more or less Walter Buckley
was bringing a load of cows
down off Cedar Mountain
he lost his brakes
come up on a State gravel truck
right on the U-turn
it was a miracle he sed
he'd done told the Lord good-bye for now
be seeing you right soon
he rammed that gravel truck
from the back
they switched loads

gravel truck dumped
right on his cattle truck
mashed in the hood
busted his windshield out and
buried him up to his chest
in gravel running out
both side winders
them cows went right over the top
his truck into the bed

of the State truck
two of them hanging out the dump feed
four with broke legs
and half a dozen jumped out
run off into the forest
never found two of them
three on their backs bellering
that driver burnt his brakes
getting that truck stopped
about a yard from the clift edge
Walter Buckley sez
you got any matches? here's
some firewood by the road
I got a sharp knife
let's have a fry if you'll unbury me
he had three broke ribs and a arm
but he lived

I'd let you drive
but you aint no better'n I am
like a monkey with a football
behind the steering wheel
look back there and see
what they doing
they jostling this truck
all over the road
tell them to be still
we almost there

September 1st

Winter's gone be here
before you known it sed John
I said yes, you can smell it in the air
can't you? but John sed no
I smoke I caint smell nothing
but I can see
it's mice turds everywhar
you turn over a board or a lid
fifteen of them jump up and run
acrost your shoes
into the other room or
toward the house

LaVerne sez she done caught a dozen
in the traps and it's more
coming in I seen them
out the corner of my eye
in ever room and she sez
she can smell them
stinking up the house
like it aint never been cleaned
and there's no cats left
Where'd they all go John? I said
I haven't seen a cat in a month

If it wasn't against the law
I'd get me a shotgun
after that Robb boy
from down to Parowan or a board
whup his ast all the way home
he got that one lion dog
his daddy's the goverment trapper

so he trained it to hate cats
taken it all over his town
turned it loose on every cat he seen
let it kill it and then
drove him in his pickup
around Midvalley and when it was a cat
he'd put that dog on it
even if it belonged to somebody else
and clumb up a tree after it
when it found one to throw him down
let that dog tear it up
Orella Lister had sixteen cats they say
which is too many
she needed them thinned
not all killed and she's only got
one left and it's one of them
Siamese twin cats that's cross-eyed
and been raised in the house
aint got sense to drink
out of a mud puddle
only thing it knows how to do
is wear a collar
and now look
it's mice everwhar

you caint get rid of them
even if he hadn't killed your cat
I put a snake in the corncrib
when I's younger
until Mama grapt it
by the neck and I haven't since
LaVerne has to set the traps
I caint stand to do it
with my fingers all stiff

it aint no way I can tell
when the spring's cocked
it goes off in my hand on my thumb
or just when I put it down
I holler and LaVerne gets mad
in the house so I say
if you don't like the noise
you do it she sez
get out of my way
I say why didn't you say so
in the first place then?
but I have to take the dead mice
out of the traps
she won't do that
they'd have to bury them right there

Why don't you get some poison,
John? I said
you can put that out
and let it do the work for you.
Oh shit, Roy Talbert did that oncet
he had mice all over his house
where he lived alone
never did get married
couldn't stand it finally
he took and bought some d-con
four boxes of it I think
set it out
went off to work
he drove truck back then
was gone four days

when he got home he's hungry
made him a sandwich

out of bananas and jelly
taken a bite and seen this mouse
laying dead on the floor
he walked through that house
looking to see forty-two mice
all dead while he's eating
his sandwich and
it turnt his stomach he sed
he taken that d-con
that was left outside
thrown it straight up in the air
as far as he could
and the rest of his sandwich

he left and slept in a motel
for a week until the rest
of them mice was through dying
he couldn't take the thought
of it no more till it was over
he went home
scraped his floors with a grain shovel
to get whatall he could out
sed for a year he'd open
a drawer or a cubbordoor or a shiffarobe
it was a dead mouse looking at him
he wouldn't have no poison
in his house if you give it to him

I wisht we could get rid of them
or get them to stay away awhile
if we don't have two more weeks
of growing season
I'm gone have four bushel of chow chow
and no tomater juice

I aint ready for winter yet
my garden aint done
and it aint even a cat to buy
around here now
him and that dog kilt them all
and look what happened

September

Evening:
the red sow
rises from her mud
to wade in
elm shadow.

Roofing the Barn

John Edward Lefler
MR 3 U.S. Navy
World War II
Feb. 19, 1917–Aug. 11, 1980

Splang bang bloing tooin
Hey, Norman, while you're down there
whyn't you take and get some more
of them leadheaded nails
I'm about out in my aporn
I got a few in my shirtpocket
LaVerne'll be calling us in
for suppertime pretty soon I bet
let's put four more pieces
of that eight-foot sheetiron on now
before we quit to eat
on this part so it'll be done
sproing goddamit
I caint get this one started
I wish they'd drilt starter holes
in it for you

Going to snow tonight John
I sed mebbe we ought not
to break for awhile longer
I can see that sed John
it's feathers coming down now
we got to hurry
if we can get this side done only
it's better'n nothing
I can crowd the sheep in over here
what about that barn

in Paragonah I heard almost burned down?
It didn't burn John,
the fire got to it but didn't
go up the side.
You wasn't there though to see?
No I sed I was out of town

We had a barn burner
back home oncet had everbody
wondering who it was setting fires
sed John Norman is that
goddam hammer down there somewhere?
What goddam hammer? sed Norman
That goddam two-pound one
I can get these nails started with
sed John did you know
that feller got killed by the truck?
Yes I did John I sed
he was a friend of mine.
It's too bad about that
what was it happened?

It was a grass fire
in Ardell Talbert's backyard I sed
this the one you want? Norman sez
John sed thow it up here
that's the one
not so damn hard you gone
hit me in the mouth with it
so what then?
It spread across his backyard
I sed and ran toward
Wanda Benson's barn so they
sounded the alarm

I know a man where I come from
sed Norman who burnt his barn down
over cats back home one time
So how'd he get killed? sed John
He didn't but the cats did sed Norman
All the firemen jumped on the truck
he was in the front seat I sed
by the driver but jumped off
to get something and
somebody got his seat
Lift me up one piece of sheetiron sed John
One of these? sed Norman
I got it I sed he wants eight-footers
so he tried to get on the back
but slipped on the concrete
the truck went over him

This guy I know sed Norman
was milking cows in his barn
name Clovis Bowen I believe
this one night with his boy there
I growed up with back then
named LeRoy Bowen for a lastname for sure
Here grab the end I sed
I got it sed John give it a push
For a long time they looked
all over to see who it was
setting them barns on fire back home
they thought mebbe it was somebody
for the insurance at first
but then it was too many
different ones so that couldn't be it
but it was all against Bryant Williamson's
insurance so they thought then

it was somebody out to get him
who's driving that truck
was it some kid?
It doesn't matter John
I sed it was an accident
John, LaVerne called from the house
supper's on the table
We coming John yelled
soon as we get this one piece done
did it kill him right then?
No I sed it smashed his pelvis
but he never lost consciousness
he was mad and screaming at the kid
who stole his seat on the truck
They was cats sed Norman
up in the eaves and rafters
of Clovis's barn he screamed at
that caused his fire
this one cat that night must of set there and
got hypmotized like they do
by the smell of that squirt
squirting in the bucket
of milk going in it
he fell over the edge
am I eating supper here or going home?
You eating here sed John
What we having then?
Probley some damn baloney sandwich
she'll holler in a minute
"it's getting cold if you don't come in"

when'd they know they
run over him?
Not until later I sed
They knew that cat come down

right then sed Norman
I bet they did sed John
it took all summer of watching
to find who's setting them fires
then they caught him at it
it was Don Baker
one of Charley Baker's idiots
carrying matches they known
he's going round burning trashbarrels
he'd built his business up
to barns by then to watch them burn
didn't have nothing to do
with the insurance one bit
John LaVerne called you coming?

Directly we be right in
hand me up anothern
they put out the fire and never known
he wasn't even there?
They said Kevin stood on the hood
of the firetruck I sed
with the bullhorn yelling into it
"I have the authority to deputize
you the on spot."
Who bought him one of them? sed Norman
"I can arrest you if you refuse to help
fight this fire," he kept saying
That cat sed Norman come down
clawing holes in the air to hold on
Lift the side up so I can grab it
sed John right there I got it
He brung down a half bale of straw
a chicken's nest and four kittycats
right on that cow's back

Chester Robertson I sed
was on the other side of the yard
telling the firemen where
to squirt their water
Did they listen to him? sed John
He's on the town council I sed
you bet they listened to him
half the town drove up
in their cars to watch
Nobody else was there that night
sed Norman except LeRoy
who his daddy had made stand up
holding the cow's tail
so he wouldn't be swatted in the face
when she tried to swoosh them flies
Don Baker was too much
of a idiot to keep flies off hisself
they couldn't do nothing to him
by law until he's eighteen years old
so he run off later sed John
almost burnt hisself up one time
hitched a ride on a truck
when he jumped off and lit on his ast
he had his buttpocket filt with matches
they caught and got him on fire
but somebody seen it and put it out

splang JOHN
I told you I'm coming John sed
soon as I get this done right now
how'd they get the fire out
with that much help there?
Ardell's wife hooked up
a garden hose and did it I sed

Where's them nails I need? sed John
I'm done out by now
Here sed Norman I been standing here
holding them for you for a hour
since you asked me to
so that cow jumped straight up
and bellered so it scairt LeRoy
he let go the tail and turned to run
she smacked Clovis his daddy in the eye
put cowshit in it where he couldn't see
jumped up him and LeRoy both
got their foot in the milkbucket
that cat screamed louder when he seen
Clovis cause he hated cats
clawed down the cow's side sliding off
kicked him in the chest
right into where he'd just shoveled
fresh cowshit to get it
out of his way so he could milk
                    bam blam

Okay get anothern up here
before LaVerne has a brainspasm
hurry up now she's getting mad
so what happened to him?
It just knocked his wind out sed Norman
Here you go I said
it took a week for him to die.
Clovis was so mad
he got his gun to shoot that cat
but couldn't find it
They couldn't find Don Baker
sed John after that for a year
then brung him back from Texas

or Arkansas where the law had him
he went to work at his daddy's
junkyard till he's eighteen
and they could put him in the state
insane asylum then they hoped
They's back in the rafters sed Norman
John this is the last time
I'm calling sed LaVerne
this food is getting cold
We coming I sed John sed

They was all meowing and squalling
he shot up a pocketful of shotgun shells
killed three chickens but no cats
Took him a week? John sed
He went into a coma
never came out of it
Well he never felt it that way
Don Baker was welting on a car
with a torch and cut
into the gas tank on it
blowed hisself all to hell
bet he got a bang out of that
When Clovis couldn't shoot them
he started hollering I'll get you
you sonofabitch I'll fix you
he went and burned his barn down
to get rid of them cats
Half the fire department I sed
didn't even go to his funeral
They didn't even have one for Don Baker
that I known of
that other sister of his
that her tongue hung out her mouth

they'd arredy tied her up insides
so she couldn't have no kids
after that carnival man
took her in the truck to show her
the snakes and knocked her up
but the baby died in her
they sed but others say
that wasn't what happened
they fixed her
when he heard about Don Baker
Dan Cockrum sed "there went
the town supply of idiots"
and Charlie Baker died of a heart attackt
somewhere about that time
The cow dried up sed Norman
she wouldn't be milked no more
I hope we finished now I'm hungry
I hope they aint no more of them John sed
I hope he didn't feel it I thought
JOHN
        we coming I sed right NOW
let's go eat
        John sed
Lord bless this tunafish sandwich
which we are about to receive
        a voice inside me breathed
Lord keep a strong roof
over all thy wayward sheep

Evening

No rest for the wicked
and the righteous don't need any

That's done up right and through
let's go have a coldbeer inside
and set on the furniture

No, John, I'm going home
I'm tired I'm going to bed
and I may not get up tomorrow
I may sleep all day

Oh no you caint do that
the auction starts at nine
they do weinerpigs first
we got to be there

I'll call you early at six
so you can sleep till then
we gotta have breakfast
and go to the auction

so you take and go on home
I'll be by to get you
in my truck
         we got work to do
we gone buy us some pigs
make us some money
starting tomorrow morning

Coda

the dew lay all night upon my branch
JOB 29:19

John, are you sure you want
to buy these weinerpigs?
That's a lot of money.

Look, you want to go partners
or not? I done told you
I'll loan you the first half
don't you remember
the insurance sed it was
a act of god
now that means god must want
us to have these pigs
or he wouldn't of acted that way
you want to piss him off
you go ahead
but you tell him I done what
I thought he wanted me to
or he wouldn't of made me this way
is that what you want?

don't let me make up your mind
but LaVerne went to church
last Sunday they told a story
something about a man looking for a job
this tornado come up
blown off his house and crops
killed all his livestock
and his wife and family

cause they didn't have no storm cellar
they sed the Lord
he was mad at that man
I guess cause he didn't have no job

he got the hives
and mebbe the jockey strap itch all over
couldn't set still for scratching
here come the missionaries
to get him
it was three of them I imagine
a Mormon, a Jehovah Witness
and probley one of them Hairy Sutras
none of them made any sense
and then anothern come
probley a Cambellite setting up
cottage meetings

he had enough
went back to church
and the Lord spoke in tongues
they grapt his head
hollered the words and healed him
found a widow womern with a family
for him and a farm on shares
as soon as he got his dues
paid up and the Lord
wasn't mad at him no more

Now I don't know
if that's a truestory or not
but do you want to take a chance
on it? I heard
the Lord gives and takes

this time he give
so I figger if we don't take
he aint gone be pleased
and I don't have no storm cellar
and haven't got time to itch
do you?
so what you gone do about it
the auction starts in five minutes
you better make up your mind
right now

Pain

for William Kloefkorn

Now how'd you do that? sed John
and I told him
about the pickup being stuck
wouldn't start
how I got mad and put my back
against the front and started it rocking
then gave all I had
heard the disks rupture
even before I felt the blue pain
pick me up and throw me
on the ground
eyeball to antenna with a red ant
that crawled up my nose
and I didn't care

I've never hurt that way I said
it was the worst pain a man could feel

Oh shit sed John it is not
you lain back down right now
how'd you like it if I taken
and pult on these tractor ropes
they got you hooked up to
wouldn't that hurt just as bad
or worst?
and what if that one fat nurse
name Martha Rae come in
pull down your covers
with her crapper pan again
sez lift up you gotta try some more

staring at you and you aint got
no underwears on?
you tell me that don't hurt some

and everbody comes in
sez well that aint so bad
mine was worst
or my brother torn his back up
like yours and he still caint walk
or he caint stand up straight
or his pecker still don't have no feeling
in it and that was twenty years ago
or the doctor come in
sez we gone have to operate on you
and everybody you known
sed don't let him cut you
you'll be cripple for life
their uncle he's in a wheelchair
every since caint do nothing
slobbers down the front his shirt
nothing below his neck works
all the doctor's fault
you won't never be the same no more.
You gone tell me that aint the worst
to hear truestories like that
and you just laying on your butt
in the bed taking up space
from people that's really sick

No that aint the worse
it aint even the worse I heard of
I'll tell you about some pain

everybody knows about that feller
set down on a crapper
at Possom Kingdom Lake
got blackwidow spider bit
on his privates and the whole end of it
come off with the poison
but I known a man
had cancer in the mouth
hurt so bad he chewed
half his tongue off before he died
got blood poison and gangrene
anothern had to chop his leg off
with a hatchet to get out
of a beartrap or he'd froze to death
died anyway in a car wreck
going to his mother's funeral
a year later so it wasn't worth it
and old Dan Walker
when his tractor wouldn't start
hit it with a sledgehammer
missed and broke his shinbone
crawled a mile to his house
and they'd unhooked his phone
cause he's behind on the bill
that's pain

but they's some
that hurts a different way
sometimes even worse
it was this boy in the fifth grade
name George Mendietta
he would of stoled his daddy's pickup
given it to you
for this one little girl name Danella Hagins

to say hello to him
but he's a Mexican and that's too bad
for him back then
so he helt it in all year
here comes Valentine day
what'd he do? goes down
to Bob Collier drugstore
taken and bought her a box
of red Valentine candy and a card
given it to her at the class party
we all remembered
cause she cried and had to go
to the nurse's office
she's so embarrassed to have a Mexican
do such a thing to her
he never come back to school
the rest of the year
I think that hurt purdy good

that aint the worse
I known of
I hurt just as bad
over Thelma Lou Shackleford
when I's seventeen
we all went out to eat fish
we'd been messing around all day
it was that night I known
I loved that girl more'n life
we all order oysters and horse relish
cept Thelma Lou
she orders catfish and the man
sez you want that broil or fried ma'am?
she sez fried
I can still hear the way that sound

slid off the front of her tongue
I's so ashamed eating raw oysters
I couldn't hardly hold one
in my mouth and Tommy Wayne Clayborn
ate his and half of mine
slopped saucet all over the table
like a hog licking his fingers
I watched her eat every bite
of her fish begging myself John
ask her to go for a ride
but I's too scared
afraid she might say no or laugh
when she's through
Tommy Wayne sez come on Thelma Lou
let's go up Sawmill Road
she never sed a word
got up and walked off with him
it wasn't nothing I could do
but watch her go

and that's not the worse
Thelma Lou was my sister's bestfriend
I known for a fact
cause Thelma Lou told her
she told me
how when she's twelve and come in
first time how she never known
what it was
nobody done told her
she thought she's busted something
bleeding to death
she went in the kitchen
told her mother
her mother never turnt around

sed you get out of this room
you shut the door behind you
caint you see I'm cooking supper
I think that's worse

but even worst than that
was Tommy Wayne Clayborn
knocked her up and I think he done it
that night I couldn't say nothing
on the Sawmill Road
they didn't know what to do
everbody in town known about it
before they got around to telling their folks
finally Tommy Wayne told
his daddy name Shirley Clayborn
he's the sheriff back then and a good one
about the toughest man in town
partly because of his name
you'd say morning Shirley
he'd look right in your eye
if it was sparkling any
it wouldn't be purdy quick
so Tommy Wayne told him
he said what you gone do, boy?
Tommy Wayne sez gone marry her, Daddy
Shirley sed is that what you want?
Tommy Wayne sez yas she's a hell of a girl
and she was goddammit
Shirley Clayborn called her family over
they all talked it out and sez okay
if that's how it is
and nobody got his ast kicked
like he should of
when they left Tommy Wayne

was just standing there in the room
with his daddy
Shirley went over and poured
two glasses of bootleg whiskey
he'd confisgated out sez you want a drink?
Tommy Wayne sed yas I do I think
and they did
then Shirley Clayborn sez
boy, do you know what's worst
than doing what you did to that girl
in the backseat of my Chevrolet car?
and he sez no Daddy, what?
Shirley Clayborn sed
not doing that to that girl
in the backseat of my Chevrolet car

and that's pain.
All my life I've had to known
I never had a daddy like that
and it aint no way I know how
to be one either
and you caint tell me you hurt worst
than I do about that

and besides
I busted my back up
like yours
and I think mine's worst
when I got home
I couldn't set up in bed by myself
so LaVerne put a screw in the ceiling
we hooked up a comealong
to help me get up and a belt
around my chest

so I needed to pee and I hit that ratchet
belt slipped down around my belly
I done comealong my back
up off the bed
I holler and here comes LaVerne
she don't know how to undo
that ratchet and let me down
she hit it three licks
there I am my head and feet
touching the bed and the rest of me
pretending to be a rainbow
with slipped disks
me needing to pee
the only way she could think of
to get me down so I'd quit hollering
was with a hacksaw
neighbors a mile off
heard me and come down fore
she got me cut loost
seen where I couldn't help it
peed all over my bed
I couldn't do nothing but
lay in it

so don't tell me about the worst pain
cause it aint never the worse
it's always something better'n that
you can bet on it anyday
besides here come the fatnurse
so you better be getting ready, now.

My Town

Prelude

You can't go home again
T. WOLFE

That's shit
BILL HOLM

Who sed that?
Did somebody say that
or was it in one of them damn books you read?

It don't matter
it's a pile of crap
I go home ever day
don't matter where I am
I'm the prodigal son coming back
I don't even need a Greyhound bus
I can go to my town right now
right here talking to you
because this
is everywhere
I've ever been

Terrace Mound

Go through them gates
and turn left

them's the Rushings
had the little grocery store
after he quit farming
and there's Maloufs
they's immigrants
spoze most of us are
they took a later boat
had this boy Tommy
with the cancer in high school
that played football
chopped him off a part at a time
had a thumb and a little finger
on that one hand
then they took his thumb
and a leg
he give it up

Kay Stokes down there
with the big fence
and the Patricks next door
them's the expensive people
Bryant Williamson down a little further
turn there

here's Edna Mae Garner and Rufus
way down there at the end
with the white picket fence is Lela's
and over there in that flat place
in the sun is Ellis Britton

should of planted a tree there
be shade for the whole block
my Lard I couldn't of told you
what Buck Gosset's name was
2 minutes ago if I hadn't seen it

down to the left
at the end of that street's
a Gypsy come in with the carnival
got in a knife fight
over one of the wormen
so he stayed

and acrost that street
right down there, see?
was a man I loved
that's Mr. Cummings's place
and up from him

Ugly

Ugliest man in town
was Raphael Martinez
he's kin to them Martinezes
I never told you about
had them triplet boys
2 born hooked together on one leg
and this sister
that grown a extra tit
right above her hip they sed
but they never cut them apart
borned dead
so they took the 2
and put them in a museum
in a jar where you
can go to see them
looking at you through the alcohol
he wasn't born that way

herded sheep up above Sawmill Road
this one morning he woke up
wished he hadn't of
couldn't stand up the pain was so bad
he known he couldn't live with it
and it was too far to town
like a weasel inside him
chewing he said
he found his pistol
put it in his mouth and pulled
bullet torn out his cheekbone
shot off half his ear
never hit no brains at all

and that was the only bullet left
he couldn't get to the rifle

so after he waited to die
and finally didn't
taken his knife
cut his throat but didn't hit a vein
stabbed hisself but the blade
was turned wrong
on a rib and bounced off
stabbed hisself higher
and harder
hit his collarbone so it broke
the knifeblade off
part of it stuck in the bone
he thrown hisself in the fire

sed that hurt too bad to stay
it was coals from last night
melted his face on one part
burnt off the hair on that one side
where it never did grown back
closed up one eye
carterized his neck
where he cut it so it almost stopped bleeding
sed he could hear hisself frying
for somebody's breakfast
but he had to roll out
couldn't stand it no more
found a shoeing hammer
took and hit hisself
hard as he could
between the eyes
with both hands on the handle

knocked him out so hard
he should of starved to death
before he woke up
but didn't
had a lump the size
of a ostrich egg growing on his face
so he had one more idea

tied a pigging rope on his feet
drug hisself to this mule he had
a mean kicking bastard
crawlt up on his back
and tied his hands to his feet
under that mule's belly
sed he never known how that mule
let him get on he's hollering so
of the pain when he moved
that mule hated being loaded
and he'd even untied him first
he could of run off or kicked him
in the mouth there on his knees
he figgered that mule
would at least thrown him off
over his butt and kick loose
cave mebbe the rest of his head in
mule turnt and went to town

got him there by afternoon
passed out
people who found him was scairt to death
seen that one side
didn't have no face left
blood all over that mule
like he'd been swatting flies on him

with a icepick
they took him to the hospital
couldn't figure out what was wrong
saw all them holes in him
burnt-off spots
blood everwhere
when they went
to lay him out straight he'd scream
like hell and they couldn't understand
a word of it
the only English he's speaking
was Spanish
couldn't wake him up enough
to shift his gear
tried to patch him up
best they could
without it costing much
they known it wasn't no insurance
nobody wanted the mule

that night they sed
he set up hollering like a sonofabitch
grapt his privates like
he'd pull it off
they taken and given him a shot
by next morning
he passed as big as the end of your thumb
this kidney stone
sed it turnt his gentile inside out
never seen one that big before
he bored a hole in it
worn it for a necklace
I seen it many a time
my god he's ugly

about half a face
with the eye shut on that side
half a ear
throat cut scar and his arms
blistered from his elbows to hands
where he lain in that fire
dent between his eyes
and a big white spot
where his cheekbone used to be
before the bullet come out
wasn't a kid in town
who'd stay on the same side of the street
as he's walking on
never bothered him a bit
he's happy as a goose
and about that many brains left

so about a year before he died
he come in to the doctor again
all wadded up in a bunch
his kinfolk brought him
give him the examination
and the X ray by then
doctor sez I got bad news for you
sed his face went as white
as a Nazarene preacher or a highway patrol
doctor sez you got the cancer
Raphael Martinez almost fell off the chair

started laughing and bawling
did the cross thing
sed oh thank god goddam thank god
I's afraid it'd be the kidney stone again
he's so happy they sed

it almost looked like that face
would of busted like a balloon
sed he wasn't afraid of no cancer
or dying cause he'd been there before
but with the kidney stone
it wasn't no way he could find out
how to not be there when it happened
and that's just too ugly
for him to have to think about

Fruit Trees

See them 4 trees out there?
They been in 8 years
haven't had one apple or pear yet
I believe that grocery store
he grafted box elder on
except that kind would of grown
them won't even do that

back home ever fall at the fair
they had a fruit judging
from whoever's trees wanted
to bring it in to be looked over
2 years in a row this Jesus Salinas
kept the graveyard mowed and watered
dug and filt graves up
planted some fruit trees in a row
won the blue ribbon
second time for peaches, apples, pears
and persimmons I think
about ever one they had

bunch of other people
pitched a hissy
sed it wasn't fair
he never owned that land
them trees was on
belonged to the county
and the dead people who paid
to be there
it wasn't one inch his
Ellis Britton never even
got a white ribbon for 5th

sez besides he's got a unfair advantage
being borned in Mexico
naturally good at it
sed it aint no way
the rest of us can get
that much fertilizer down that deep
he sez youg'n either pick anothern
by god I'll go out there
and chop every damn tree
in the graveyard down
it won't be no fruit or shade
left for nobody out there
to lean up against waiting
I don't have to put up
with this one minute
you caint take away
my taxpaying rights

judge had to start over
pick a fair winner
they'd all agree to and make sure
Ellis got some kind of ribbon
after it was over sed
when he died they ought to plant
a bannanar tree on Ellis Britton's grave
enough fertilizer
to put Cuba out of business
if it didn't burn the tree up

them of mine
got one more year
if it aint no fruit
I aint driving very far
to get some firewood
that's a fact

Preacher

In 1956 Babtists got a new preacher
Reverent Pastor Brother Strayhan
from the Southern Tennessee preacher school seminary
he had a Bible they give him
for graduating had about 40 ribbons
marking his page number
hanging out the back
every color you could imagine
after he'd been there about a year
still tell them about how
they didn't appreciate him enough
because he was awarded them ribbons
for being outstanding in his field
one day Mizrez Bouchier
who was old enough to not care no more
sed after church she wished
he'd go back and stand
out in his field some more
she had enuf of him arredy

he'd preach swinging that thing
round like a Chinerman's kite
by the end the sermon
he'd took out the ribbons marking spots
all worked up to give the invitation
swung it so hard oncet
them ribbons chopped the top
off a incarnation in the pulpit flowerpot

he loved to preach on how
he got calt by the Lard to be his servant
when he's only 16 years old

met his lovely wife that same summer
my mama sez she figgered he's right
all boys that age get calt
some of them even on the telephone
but she thought the Lard
got a wrong number that time
we all scrut up now and then

he had about 9 kids
sed it was the Lard's will
oldest one not even 12
his wife looked like a inner tube
without about half its air
you'd hear her in the grocery store
2 aisles over
her feet drug so
she's wore out not even 30
and known it was her
before you saw her
by the sound

even if he got his preacher pay
and a house and a car
and his electric and water
with all them kids he thought
it wasn't enough to get by on
every 3d Sunday the sermon
was on the collection plate
and the bread on the water
he'd go round town
asking all the business for a preacher discount
wouldn't buy nothing in a store
if they didn't mark it down for him
when they didn't

he could make them sorry for it
he'd find some way to get it
into one of his sermons
whole churchhouse would go
somewheres else after that
whether they believed it or not
his kids got in the pitchershow
half price and free meals
at the school lunchroom
and the ball games without paying
because it was the Lard's will

so oncet he went to Lela's cafe
for supper with his whole family
stood there at the counter
before he'd set down
sed how much is your menstral discount
to eat there
customers listening 2 waiting to pay
sez I need at least 20 percent?
Lela sed whar? she wasn't even
a Babtist but a Presbyter
sez my family and I get discounts
because of I'm the Babtist Reverent
of up to half at most places
one of the people eating there
Clovis Robinson I think
sed yes ma'am that's a fact
he's a Babtist deacon
had to back him up without no choice
wasn't nothing she could do
everbody watching to see
if they'd all walk out
Lela sed set down

I'll do my 20 percent one time
all them kids standing there
with their mouths hanging open
3 of them didn't even
have their britches zipped up

he ordered tunafish sandwiches
and a glass of water
for all them kids because it was cheapest
fried chicken for his wife
because that was most for the money
and told this waitress
to bring him a steak to eat
how do you want that cooked? she sed
Scriptural he sed
she sed what?
he sez well done
my good and faithful servant
leant back and grint
proud of hisself like he thought
she ought to brang him a dish of icecream
for free for thinking that up

Lela heard it
hollered through the window
from the cash register to the cook
whole cafe listening
fix that preacher's kids hamburgers
with french fries
make his wife shrimps and whitefish
put him a steak on
from off the bottom of the pile
I'll pay the different
cook sez how he want that steak?

she yelled Scriptural
burn that sonofabitch to hell
he never did come back there
to eat again after that
and it never hurt Lela's business
not even one bit

Deaf

for Margaret Christensen

Clovis Walker had this uncle
by marriage who went deaf
when he was about 40
they sed it was shooting firecrackers
when he's a boy out of season
but he sed they lied
he only did it July too
except for that one year
when they fount them blasting caps
it run in his family
his daddy couldn't hear neither

when he's 52
he was feeding his sow with pigs
she whirlt round and bit
half his hand off
where he had a thumb
and 2 fingers left
she swallered the rest
he sed he seen her smacking
her lips on it
couldn't hear a thing
he always wondered
if he could of heard
mebbe he'd known she's gone
bite him off like that
grunting loud to scare him off
but it wasn't no warning for him

so he was in his 60s
forgot anybody else
could hear either
he'd set in his chair at night
by the fireplace staring at it
listening backwards to hisself
rub that hand and say out loud
that goddam sow. That goddam sow.

Doc

Doc Kitchens told me
about this trapper he took the appendix out of
name Robb Valton
the one got his finger cut off
but he found it
put it in his pocket
when he got home
sewed it back on the stump part
didn't work
fell off after a week
so he buried it
but his dog smelt it
and dug it up
had it on the porch that night
green gnawing on it
sed he kicked that dog
all the way under his truck
off that porch
it turnt his stomach

so before that
when he's younger
before he even had a truck
he's up in the hills
working his lines
got this bellyache
so bad he couldn't stand up
had to crawl back
thought he'd die for sure
but it was a miracle
some 12-year-old boys
up there in his line shack

broke in looking for stills
to steal sugar from and sell
and mebbe some whiskey
they could get drunk on
or if it was bad
go blind and be famous
he caught them in there
blocked off the door
sed I'll kill you right now
and make a lampshade
out the skin off your butt
or one of you can go get Doc Kitchens
and tell him I'm bad off
while the otherns stay here till dark
and then I'll kill you anyway
if whichevern's not back by then

they commenced to bellering
so bad he sed
get out of here right now
I caint stand that
but one of you tell Doc
I need help
and if you don't I'll find you in the night
that's a fact

they's ascairt
run all the way to town
2 of them bawled the whole way
thought he's follering
but the othern did what he sed

Doc Kitchens sed
is it sumin busted?

boy sez I don't think so
he stood up and wave his arms
Is it snakebite?
No he wasn't slobbering
Was it blood?
No I never seen none
Damn he's poisoned
or the kidney stone he sed
and I only got 2 bottles of whiskey
he saddled his horse
took off

Robb Valton he's laying on the floor
in a bunch when Doc Kitchens got there
hollering oh I'm gone die
Doc sez sit up so I can see what's wrong
sed oh I'm gone die
sez sit up goddammit
or I'll whup your ast with a board
he got up and set on the table
Doc did a examination and sez
by god you got the appendicitis
Robb Valton sez is it any pills
I can take for it?
Doc sez no I'm gone have
to operate and get her out
Oh I'm gone die he said

Doc sed he sez here
you take and drink this
fast as you can
give him one bottle of whiskey
started boiling the water
got in the drawer and pulled out

all the knives
set down on the furniture
with a whetstone
started sharpening

Robb Valton drank that bottle
but couldn't get drunk
sed isn't it no more whiskey?
Doc sez here you do this
you're better'n I am at it
given him the knives to get sharp
he went to get the othern

they sharpened and Rob Valton drank
until he finally stopped and sed
you gone use these on me?
Doc sez yas I am
and the duller it is
the more you gone feel it
he sed in about 2 minutes
them knives was sharp enough
to shave a porcupine
and Robb Valton looked drunk
so he sed lay down on the table
and take your pants off

tied him down with a rope
top to bottom where only his head could move
sed try to go to sleep
so you won't feel nothing
that knife was sharp
had him open in a second
and half looking for it
about had a spasm

sed he couldn't find that appendix
in there nowhere
he got scairt wondered
if he'd cut the hole on the wrong side
and if he made 2 holes
Robb Valton would kill him
the next day for sure
he was as big as a boar hog
drunk or not
Robb Valton he lifted up his head
sed you cut me yet?
Doc sez no just shaving the hair off
he sed then let me up first
I gotta pee
Doc sez oh it's too late for that
I's lying you're open
he sed oh god I'm gone die
hollered, pissed all over the table
then like a ruptured volcano
puked straight up in the air
hollering at the same time
oh god I'm gone die
covered the walls and floor

Doc sed it was like
a stick of dynamite went off
in a rope factory
it was guts come spewing
out that hole everwhere
sed he's grabbing with both hands
and had his knee up on his chest
trying to hold them all down
wished he'd been borned a octopus
intestines wallering all over

Robb Valton bawling yelling
oh I'm gone die then puking
straight up in front of him
right there it was
that appendix all green
sticking up like a thumb
he grapt it and had it down
on the table and off
then had to get it all
shoved back in
sed he never imagined a elephant
had that many in there
but Robb Valton helped by passing out
he sewed him up
didn't even have a shot to give him

put the appendix
in a mason jar of whiskey to keep
so he could take it home
to put on a shelf and look at
had him a drink
and went to sleep
setting up in a chair watching
to see if he'd die

sed first thing he remembered
was Robb Valton shaking him
arredy had coffee on
sez you sonofabitch
you sewed some scissors or pliers
up inside me
it's sumin in there hurts
never would tell him
how he got untied from that table

sed for years
every time he'd see him
Robb Valton'd pull his pants down
and show where Doc Kitchens
cut him open with a axe
and sewed him up with baliwore
ever kid in town seen that scar

he's the only doctor we had
and got his degree out the back
of a funny book they sed
until they built the hospital
and got a real one
he had to retire
and go to horses and dogs
in the shed behind his house
but Mama told me
he was the first person to slap my ast
so I figger he must of
been worth something
I known Robb Valton
sed he'd of been dead many a time
if it wasn't for Doc Kitchens
but he sure as hell wished
he'd of been there
when he needed him for that finger

Bryant Williamson

Onriest man in town I guess
was old Bryant Williamson the 1st
that was his boy's and
his boy's name too the 2nd and 3d
in a row with the same name
he's rich
made his seed money in the oil
off his ranch

he put part of that oilmoney
in a insurance business
he had a brother in the goverment
known what was coming up
how the goverment was gone make
everybody buy the insurance
he got in
before it caught on
was a millionaire back then
when it was worth something
from the oil and the insurance both

he's smart and sent them boys
to school to be lawyers
teach the people
how to sue each other
so he could sell more insurance
when they got sued for protection
had the law office right there
the insurance next to it
with a door in between
and a doorbell on both
so one of them could run it

at a time and the rest could be
doing something else
everthing they did made money

after he's rich he didn't care
what nobody thought
he had enough money to mind
whoever's business he wanted to
or not his own if he felt like that
whatever's on his mind
didn't stay in it he sed it out loud

oncet the radio station called him
sez is this Bryant Williamson?
he sed who the hell
you think it is? you called me
I never touched the telephone till it rung
radio sez Mr. Williamson
you on the air
he sed is that a fact?
radio sez yas and the reason
we calling is you just bought
a new Ford from Ed Power Fordhouse
and we want you to tell
the listening public in your own words
how much you appreciate
that new Ford from Ed Power's

he sed in my own words
that is the sorriest goddam
piece of machinery anybody
every put on a set of wheels
since they invented Mack trucks
I'm thinking about

putting one of Charley Baker's idiots
in it and driving it off a cliff
saying he stoled it for the insurance
I wouldn't drive that thing
to a damn goatroping contest
and if somebody wants to take Ed Power
out and shoot him in the head
I'll buy the bullet
he's one lying cheap snotnose sonofabitch
you can quote me in the newspaper
I'll buy the advertisement

it was a highschool boy
running the radiostation that day
following orders
didn't know how
to turn him off
it went on the radio
we all heard it except Ed Power we guessed
he never sued him
we thought for sure he would
but he wouldn't of won
the only lawyers that was suers
was Williamsons then

he had to go to the doctor
for a specialist up to the capital oncet
his boy the 2nd drove him
they went by the college on the way
at this stoplight
college boy in a red car
that looked like a football player
pulled up beside him
Bryant Williamson leaned out

and spit Brown Garrett snuff all on his face
in his red car with the top down
that boy jumped out
would of put dents on his head
but Bryant Junior the 2nd
run over and stopped him
sed look we sorry
he's a old man you can see that
look at him he never meant that
it was a accident
here take this handkerchief of mine
it's a new one cost 2 dollars
you wipe that off and keep it
it's yours you don't owe me nothing
that boy calmed down
sed all right but I don't like that
one bit you better get him out of here
Bryant the 2nd sed I am
I'm taking him to the doctor
right now he don't see too good
that's what's the matter

he got back in
old man Williamson sed
the sonofabitch should of
had his winder rolt up
before that boy could get out
Bryant pulled in the off lane
run the red light and turned left
on a one-way street wrong
honking his horn to get away
he wasn't gone have nobody
whup his ast over that

so when he died
they read his will it sed
I caint take my money with me
but I can take my fish
he wouldn't let nobody fish
on his place
him and Beulah K. Byrd
had a advertisement in every Thursday paper
no hunting fishing or trespassing
on my ranch signed their name
Beulah on hers had
survivors will be persecuted by the law
she drove around in a jeep
with a 410 shotgun looking for you
she'd shoot if she seen you
on her land but Williamson
hired a Mexican to look for him
so after they buried him
they went to all his stocktanks
thrown 3 sticks of dynamite in it
every one and killed all the fish
by god just to show he could do
whatever he wanted to
with anything that was his

Clean

Are your garments spotless,
are they white as snow,
are you washed in the blood of the Lamb?
CHRISTIAN HYMNAL NUMBER TWO

Cleanest womern that every lived
was Mizrez Bullard
her kids' ears bled she scrubbed so hard
even on Wednesday night prayer meeting
and after she warshed clothes
in her house on Thursday
she'd use the warshing machine water
to mop the porch and the sidewalk
and the street curb all clean

then her husband before he ran off
brought home this white cat
for the kids he named Nookie
so after she did those clothes and sheets
on Thursdays she's so clean
she warshed that cat

it never went out of the house
but on Thursdays when she got out
the warshing machine
you could see it through the window
trying to scratch a hole out
then by afternoon when she's finishing clothes
it'd be a white streak
across the floor one room to another

every one of her kids ran off and left
before they got out of school
and her husband with another womern
she still warshed everything in the house
every Thursday and that cat
it wasn't no chance for it to get away
she had one thing on her mind
and anything it was dirty
didn't have no place in there to hide

you'd hear her looking for it
hollering here Nookie Nookie, come here kitty
a block away you'd know
when she found it by the squall
her arms had scratch marks
all the way up but she never felt a thing
by god, her and that cat was clean

Fast

Janie Grace Gosset could outrun anybody
in the high school back then
before she had that car wreck
if she'd of been born a boy
she could of been on the football team
except she's probley too little
her whole body was one piece of muscle
like a carpenter's crowbar
welded together without even a joint
you could of struct a match on her
you don't believe me?
a gopher match, anywhere

she'd wear bluejeans to the school on Fridays
like all the girls did oncet
it looked like two boar hogs in there
fighting it out in a chicken coop
when she walked past you with them britches on
Edgar McMahon down to the gin
sed if he could get cotton that tight
he'd put a 800-pound bale in a tow sack

then she took up with that sorry Haroldwayne Johnston
before he went blind and started being a gospelpreacher
he slobbered all over her
for about a half a year
until he ruint her reputation so he'd have a excuse
to move on to anothern
they sed she's going 80 miles a hour at least
when she went off the caprock
after he done it all and told

it was this one springtime
they's having the highschool track meet
whole town come out to see
if she could outrun Jimmy Ray Gary
who was gone graduate and go to the college
be on the team there
they had all the other races first
so we'd have to wait and see
finally it come to the last one
there she was in it
wearing this tight pink running outfit

that gun went off
first half she was out in front good
then he pulled up, all the otherns
was done behind by then
them 2 right beside each other the last part
everybody there was struck deaf and dumb
like they's on the road to Damascus
their mouths hanging open like it was a vision
for just a second or 2 that day turned into pear jelly
her body melted into that running suit
looked like she was bald naked running wide open
only othern seemed to be moving
besides them 2 was Haroldwayne Johnston
running down to the finish line to grab her
like she's a Holstein cow right in front of everybody
probley thought she done all that just for him

I don't think anybody could tell you
who won that footrace
we lost it in the watching
but we all had words for it
that we known by heart

I heard my mouth say Amazing Grace
we all remember R.B. McCravey hollering
that there's poetry in motion
Ollie McDougald sed it was a religious experience
but Leonard Tittle who was arredy preaching on weekends
and had both of them in his class of algebrar
sez right out loud
nosir gentlemen you are all wrong
that was Grace abounding to the chief of sinners

Potts Coal Mine, Inc.

Brother Coy Stribling
finally got this job
working in the coal mine
he'd been fired
from everything else
except preaching at the ChurchofGod
that believed in flags
didn't make enough
to get by on
he'd about hit bottom
when he got hired

hadn't been working there
a week when it was a cave-in
right when he was telling them
about the Ethiopian eunuch
about a half mile down
felt the mountain shake
heard it grunt
they run back up
it's closed off
sealt in

stood there a minute
staring at that slide rock
Coy Stribling sez
brethern let us pray
he started the preacher prayer
nobody could understand
about the mysteries of the Lard
and the faith in the churchhouse
Jimmy Don McCampbell sed

goddam I smell gas
let's dig
all them miners took after
that rock pile
like a chainsaw
slinging it everywhere

Coy Stribling he seen
finally it wasn't nobody listening
so he gave it up
and even he started digging
some said it was only time
anybody ever seen him
turn a hand
they's ascairt
nobody down there thought
they might not
get out of that one dead

dug till some of them
was bleeding up both arms
some bawling
others hollering
to keep them all working
never known how long
they'd been at it
batteries in their headlights run out
it wasn't no time down there
dark as Jonah's whale
and then they broke through

it was a little hole
but they could smell the air
and known if they messed with it

whole thing might cave in
they took a chance
one at a time crawlt through
skinny ones first
fat ones ready for Brother Coy
to stop preaching
about the camel's eye and the needle
but they didn't have to tell him
every one of them made it
through that hole
him 3d from last
some had scrape marks on their ribs
looked like a hogfight
but they's through and running

got up that tunnel and out
no more'n set down
to get a count
that mountain farted
squat down and took a shit
mud and gas and rocks
come out that hole
like a tornado's tearing out
but no fire
thrown rock
over half a mile
down the canyon
knocked ever one of them
ast over appetite
and Junior Bechamp busted his arm
didn't even know it
till the next day
but not one of them
got killed

Coy Stribling
when it was through
all settled down
and they saw they's all alive
stood up and sed
would you like to sing a hymn, brethern?
R.B. McCravey sed
would you shut the fuck up, Coy?
he set down
never said another word

They's there for a hour
in the night
nobody moving or saying nothing
waiting for morning
when the rescue party come up
from town to find the bodies
they'd heard the blow-up
known everbody in that mine was dead
walked right up on them ·
without seeing them setting there
J.R. Potts sez whar's the mine
I caint see it?
Jimmy Don McCampbell sed
it's right over there but it's sealt off
J.R. Potts about died
of the heart attack
he sez goddam you
you like to ascairt me to death
where are you?
and they shined the light on them
you posta be all dead he sed
how come you setting round like that?
Coy Stribling sed we watching

in the garden
with the Lard, brother
R.B. McCravey was ready to kill him
but he just sed kiss my ast, Coy

they opened that mine
back up in one week
almost everybody
who was in there that day
went back to work
except for a couple and
Coy Stribling
he sed he'd seen enough
he'd find something else to do
after that and he
wouldn't never get inside no hole again
as long as he lived
and his wife sed bless the Lard
for that at least
he sed not in the ground
until they buriet me
and she sed oh that
got a job at the grocery store

they cleared out all that rock
put in new timber
and had her bored and stroked
to the end in 2 months
back on schedule
J.R. Potts sed that mine was as safe
as a schoolhouse
he'd certify so hisself
and all them men sed
the mountain felt settled down

like she'd got rid
of whatall's on her mind
they didn't have no more troubles
or a accident
for almost a year after that
everbody figured
it might of been worth it
to get him that job
at the grocery store

Lazy

Laziest man ever was Floyd Scott
it wasn't nothing that boy
would ever do for anybody
when he's 5 years old
arredy too late his mama one day
sez Floyd come take this trash out
to the barrel but he just lain there
in the living room on the furniture
so she sez you taking this trash out
like I told you?
he never answered she sed
you want to take this trash out
to the barrel or do you want a whupping?
he sez finally how many licks?
she sed 3 with the flyswatter
he didn't say nothing for a minute
she thought he's coming to get it
then he sed do I have to
come out there or will you come
give it to me in here?

When he's about 12
they had supper one night called him
to come set down at the table to eat
he sed he wasn't hungry yet
they sed you don't have to eat then
he sed he was arredy there
he might as well wait till he felt like it
set there 3 hours with his elbows
on the table waiting to get hungry
they hadn't put their windowscreens
up yet and it was hot, windows open

his mama come to check on him
his face swolt up like a pomegranate
mosquitoes eat him up
couldn't even closed his mouth
had 3 mosquito bites on his tongue
too lazy to get up and move
he sed it was their fault
he calt for somebody to come close that winder
they had the television up so loud
he couldn't holler above it
it wasn't polite to get up
from the table before he's through eating

got him a job with his in-laws
where they couldn't fire him cause he's family
he wasn't worth a damn
tried to get him to string fencewore
left him there one morning
they come back to get him for dinner
he's still standing there with his hands
in his pockets staring at that wore
come up and touch him on the shoulder
he jumped straight up with his eyes open
sez goddam you snuck up on me
when I's studying how to unroll
all that wore out straight for 4 hours
give him a shovel to dig with
he leaned on it till he had a dent under his chin
had to go to the doctor to see
if the bottom of his tongue ruptured
for years when they wanted a shovel
they'd say bring me Floyd's dragline here

had to promote him to a desk job
for setting a bad influence on the other hired hands
give him the job of making coffee and answering telephone
he wouldn't even do that
his mama'd bring him to work and make it for him
had to buy a answering machine
he sed every time it rung he was always busy
checking the coffee or setting in the toilet

he was 24 years old when he
went and got in the car to drive
down to the grocery store a block away
to get him a can of beer
had this terrible itch that was a tragedy
he stretched up to scratch his ast
hit the curb and rolled the car
on flat ground right over
Doctor sed he couldn't find
nothing wrong with the X ray
but his back wasn't strong enough
for him to walk on it after that
insurance bought him 4 different wheelchairs
all too hard for him to use
till they got one with a electric motor on it
he sed he was satisfied
never walked a hundred steps in a row after that
some days he sed it was too hard and not worth the effort
to even get out of bed to it
so he got a television set in his bedroom
to help him get by on social security
that same year 4 kinds of welfare
and the AssemblyofGod brought his supper
on all days with an R in them

county paid for him a private nurse
because he sed it was a soft spot
in that pavement caused his accident
of their negligence and behavior
he was gone sue the county
and the town for a million dollars
if they didn't take care of him till he got well
they thought it'd be cheaper to buy him a nurse
for however long it took
after 3 years she found a way to get married to him
and still have the county pay her for being a nurse's helper
bought them a trailerhouse they put in
right next to his daddy's house
where he didn't have to pay no rent
after that she give up her other patients
and kept the county money for watching him
it was enough to get by on they sed

she's almost as lazy as he was
I heard moss grown in her toilets
they put a deep freezer out on the front porch
to hold the TV dinners she fixed
on all days without a R
both of them got so fat they had to have 2 couches
in the living room to set and watch TV on
so lazy a dog couldn't live with them
it'd of starved to death waiting
for one of them to come feed it

The Sawmill Road

We got our town supply
of cripples on the Sawmill Road
it wasn't a year or a season
went by that somebody didn't get
mashed up one way or anothern
on that road

it started about a mile
out of town and went straight up
to Blowup where the first sawmill was
and the boiler exploded years ago
killing 2 men and one
they never found
either blowed all to hell
or left without sending word
it's not a flat place on that road
youg'n speak of anywhere
hard going up or down
and dangerous
a lot of people got killed
and their bones busted
on the Sawmill Road

back then when wagons
was what we had
it was always a runaway
or a accident about to happen
somebody got ruint for life
Charlie Ivie was coming
downhill loaded with 2 ton of cutwood
for a barn when his neck yoke busted
wagon rode up on the horses

pushed them ahead of it
going straight down
and this drag he made
out of some logs he chained up
to the back
to slow it down come loose
his brakes wouldn't hold
wagon pushed the horses
off the road heading right for a cliff
Charlie Ivie give it up
jumped off but caught his foot
in the brakerope
it thowed him under
crushed his legs
where one had to be cut off
other one wouldn't bend
he's a sorry damn mess from then on
but the wagon turned on its own
the horses wasn't killed
they saved the wood
but he had to sell it
he couldn't build no barn after that

Ray Evans's daddy took a load
uphill to sell it to the mill
he had Ray with him
he's about 14 back then
horse stumbled
wagon started to roll back
so his daddy yelled
to jump down off them logs where he's setting
and block off the wheel
Ray couldn't find no rock close by
quick so he shoved his foot under

he sed he wouldn't do that again
mashed it flat like a duck
waddled like a fat womern
on that side from then on

the one we's all ascairt of
got Clarence Murphy
the pole strap that fits
over the neck yoke fastened
to the britchens on the harness
to keep the wagon from rolling ahead
and for backing it up
finally broke
and his brakes wouldn't hold
he jumped and got tangled
wagon went over his chest
left him splattered all over the road
turned sideways and rolled
killed one horse and broke the othern
he had to be shot
nobody got crippled though
they had to get him all in a cotton sack
to bring him down

it was right below that place
my brother and me
found that branch
and the still where
he got his finger chopped off
in the leaf springs of a wagon
stealing sugar
but it didn't make him no cripple

my uncle Elwood was going up
tandem with Cletus Young

to the sawmill when he seen
this waspnest hanging on a tree limb
he got up and crawled back
along the reach and whacked it
with a axe handle
whipped them horses with a rein
for a ways and pulled off
the side the road
here comes Cletus Young standing up
on the double tree of his wagon
them horses running belly to the ground
with a string of wasps following
like he's dragging a plow
went right on past
when he outrun them he come back
hit my uncle Elwood oncet
so hard he's knocked out
busted 2 teeth but he sed
it was worth it
Cletus got stung in his ear
sed it got him down deep
and he couldn't hear out of it no more
but we never believed him

we had a lot of hunting accidents
on that road where we'd go
for turkeys and deer
R.B. McCravey's one boy was hunting
on his horse with R.B.'s rifle
without permission
this deer run out
he had that rifle in his lap
lifted it up and fired too fast
without sighting he shot
that horse in the back of his head

when it fell down it trapped him
his one leg broke
where he limped from then on
and his hand with the rifle in it
was under him and the horse
and the saddle
smashed it up where it never did
work right after that
he wore a glove on it
couldn't even hold a cigarette
or write his name

Cephas Bilberry was hunting
rabbits up there
when he thought he seen
these turkeys out of season
he climbt through this fence
to get them and poached hisself
shot off half his chin and part of his face
a handful of teeth and one eye
on that side
he walked down that mountain
all the way home
sed he was afraid he might of
bled to death
but it never got a good start
figured mebbe the heat off the shotgun
sealed it off shut
he was a sight after that
couldn't even let him
pass the collection plate
the contribution would go down
ever Sunday he did

after we started driving cars
it was about a wreck a month
at first till we got used to it
then down to a few every year
some dead
like the Clarys that went off
Left Hand Canyon
or old man Benson that run
into a logging truck
he was too old to drive
should of known better

when he's young
before he got blinded by lightning
Haroldwayne Johnston was up there
on a Saturday night
in the backseat with Marva Beth Williamson
the hand brake must of slipped
or they got to rocking
it come out of gear
that car rolled a quarter of a mile backwards
hit a tree and broke her back
she's so skinny she could of
walked up to a flagpole
and bit a piece off
without turning her head sideways
so it might not of hit that hard
Haroldwayne sed he never known
a thing till it hit
sed he was amazed by it all
she's paralyzed for a while
but got better
walked like a goose from then on
but she's so skinny

we never noticed it
we didn't look at her that much

there's not a foot of that road
don't remember somebody by name
Carla Prowst got 5 unmarried kids up there
named every one
after its daddy
we lost a banker and a Babtist deacon
and a deputy sheriff over that road
every time she went up
we'd watch to see
who left town

when the ambulance come from that direction
we known it was a bad one
we'd wait a day to see
if Edna Mae worn her golden shoes
then we'd call the hospital
to see who and how bad
the whole town got infected
by that road
it wasn't hardly nobody
man or womern who grew up there
who didn't lose something sometime
on the Sawmill Road
we even wondered oncet
if we oughta close it off
but the town board decided if we didn't have
our Sawmill Road cripples
we'd be too perfect
and that's a load
that's too heavy to carry

No Lazy S Ranch

1

KEEP OUT

NO TRASSPASSING

POSTED

DONT COME

KEEP THIS GOD DAM GATE CLOSE

2

Kay Stokes had more money than God
he had this one grandboy
that was the football player
went on to the college to do it
in high school
man sed he had to take this class
in algebrar from Leonard Tittle
before he was being a preacher
his breath was too bad
that Patrick boy was too rich
to have that in his ear
if he needed help
it would hang there
you'd have to go to the bathroom
warsh that smell off
so he sed no he wouldn't
he could arredy count to 800
that was enuf to count his oilwells
and on a good day
all 4000 cows on the No Lazy S Ranch
he didn't need no algebrar
and Kay Stokes sed if he did
he'd buy him one to do it

he could play some football
besides having money
and ordering people around
and making sure nobody
ever set foot on his private property
without his permission which he wouldn't give
to the President of the United States
or the Catholic Pope if he was a Englishman
the only thing he ever took a inarrest in
was watching that boy play football
he offered to buy some professionals
to come play on that team for him
high school wouldn't let him
sed it was against the rules
he went to the school board
to get them to fire the principal
because the football coach
sed it might be a good idear
if he was willing to do it

didn't work
they sed he didn't need to
that team was gone win all its games
without no illegal help or otherwise
sed they's afraid the stands would cave in
so many people would come
watch that boy
Kay Stokes had this other idear
paid the money to have this fence
built all around the football field
6 foot high with barbwore on top
to make sure everybody paid to get in
he sed it wasn't no white trash
or otherns gone watch that boy play

without buying no ticket
he'd see to that at least
school made enough money
selling football tickets to build a addition
on the superintendent's house
and buy the football coach
a new car
so it was worth it they sed

school taken and given
him a celebration to thank him
for that fence that sold all them tickets
made him a sign
to go on the wall with his name on it
in a picture frame
had a assembly with all the kids there
and the teachers and the parents
and the superintendent and the football coach
and the first Christianchurch preacher
about 9 speeches telling the world
what a fine rich man he was
and a churchhouse prayer to thank Godamitey
for Kay Stokes
that grandboy up on the stage with him
then asked him if he wanted
to speak a few words for the occasion

he set there staring
for a minute
stood up and sed it's 2 things
I have to say
number one I accept this here award
on behalf of Jesus Christ
and the No Lazy S Ranch

and number 2
I bought me a Mexican
it caint read or hardly speak no language
to drive round the fences
on my ranch and I sed to shoot
on sight anybody traspassing on my property
after first making sure it aint me
or has my written permission
which it caint read
so if you aint my twin brother
keep your ast off my land
you want to fish
you go see that sonofabitch Bryant Williamson
he aint done one damn thing
for this town
not one of his kids
could be on that football team
you tell him I sed so
he set down and waited for them to clap
so that's what they did

3
his hired hands
would of rather had the burning bush
tell them they castarated the wrong bull
than have Kay Stokes get out the rag on them
his word was the Law
and if he fired them they might as well
leave the county
if they committed suicide
wouldn't nobody bury them
they'd feed them to Wesley Steven's hogs

oncet he seen these 2 setting down
snuck up behind them
to hear if they's saying something about him
but they's on wormen that day
saved their life probley
sed I suspicion you boys
done need something to do
one couldn't say nothing he's so suprised
othern sez yessir that's just what
we was getting ready to talk about
he sed you both of you go get a shovel
and right out there beside the road
where I can see you
start digging a hole
until I say stop
he known 2 foot down
they'd hit some caliche
like digging through a Republican's opinions
he went to town in his pickup

forgot them boys
didn't come back
till the next afternoon
they had this hole 12 foot deep
taking turns digging
the othern'd haul the dirt up
with a bucket on a rope
one couldn't swim
he's praying they didn't hit no water
othern was saying
just kick your legs
stay on top if it comes
I'll try to get a rope on you
make sure your head don't get down

you'll drownd for sure
othern's so worried he's sweating
and they'd got through
being tored a long time ago
Kay Stokes pulled up
looked in that hole
sed that's about good
go 9 more inches and then
do one on the other side
the same size
drove right on by
one hired hand had to wrap his hand up
in his handkerchief
blisters done all broke
they hadn't even stopped
to have no breakfast or supper
they's so ascairt of him

called California on the telephone
they mailed him 2 redwood trees
put them in them holes for gateposts
and a board acrost the top for a marker
about 40 foot high
sez NO LAZY S RANCH
NO HUNTING OR FISHING BY PERMISSION ONLY
YOU AINT WELCOME

4

he put him up a fence
running 2 miles straight
out of fenceposts cut off the limbs
of boardarc trees
when it rained them boardarc fenceposts
come alive and started being trees

almost ever one of them grown up
he sed he believed that must of been
the tree in the Garden of Eden
preacher sed no
that tree had a apple in it in the Bible
Kay Stokes sez that's what happens
when you aint got no good help
they caint even get the story
wrote down the way it happened
like anybody with common sense could see
he called the elders in
they fired that preacher
they all sed they didn't think
he wasn't no good neither
it was time for him to leave
it didn't matter
he bought them anothern

5

he had a heart attack
so bad it busted out both his eardrums
and his eyes bugged out
worse than Eugene Cummings
when he died in his pigpens
doctor told his wife
it wasn't nothing he could of done
if he'd been standing there
with a shot needle in both hands
he imagined he never felt a thing
but she sed she imagined he did
he sed he was tired of the drought
it hadn't rained in a year
had to haul the cattle water
and the fish tanks dried up

so nobody was even trying to get them
wasn't even no poachers to worry about
he sed he didn't even care about ranching no more
if it wasn't gone rain
he'd lost the taste
unless he could figure out
something to do about it
2 days after his funeral
it started to rain
they sed and there's some
who'll swear on this by god
on the 3d day of rain
in the one stocktank
over to the blue gate
it was this catfish
looked like 4 pounds
wallering in that tank
wasn't enough water to cover it up
come up through the mud
where it'd buried itself waiting
some sed it was a miracle
Mizrez Stokes sed she didn't
find it surprising at all

6

year later some people
from the town had this petition
to have the family take down
them signs and open up
the No Lazy S Ranch to public fishing
brought it to Ruby Patrick's house
which is his daughter
to give to Mizrez Stokes

she sed as long as it is one drop
of her daddy's blood
alive in anybody's veins
for as long as it takes
or that family sold that ranch
or until they could get
bannanar to grow in the pastures
and teach the cows to peel them and eat them
them signs her daddy put up
would stay right there
and he promised them Mexican fenceriders
a job for life as long
as they never learnt no language
to keep all foreigners out
and it wasn't up to her
to break no promise

that was almost 30 years ago
No Lazy S hands still paint
that fence around the football field
ever year silver in the fall
all them boardarc trees are still there
and I'll bet that catfish
weighs 40 pounds
and is still alive down in that tank
because even the Lard
wasn't gone argue with Kay Stokes they sed
it had to rain right now
or he'd have to find him another job

Interlude

Help me right here sed John
and I grasped the bottom rim,
we lifted the barrel into the pickup
then sat on the tailgate, hot,
a warm canyon breeze
spilled across the yellow grass

It was this one summer back home
I's young about the time most kids
getting out of school
but I'd done quit
old man Cummings
had me helping him lifting all this heavy weight
on a wagon load
we made a tote and set in the shade to rest
he must of started remembering
commenced to talking sez

summer clover jingle jangle

he done taken and put his hand
in his pocket and pulled out this silver dollar
looked at it like he never seen it before
smooth so you couldn't even tell
the man on the side, all the words
rubbed off from being carried so long
it was meadow clover all over
stretching out green and yellow
I didn't say nothing, he talked, sed
I was 17 they come in wagons
putting on Gypsy carnivals
whole town wanted them to go on

known they'd steal whatall's loose
everbody went to the tent that night anyway
they paid me a dollar to water horses
I worked all afternoon hard
I was 17 for a dollar

she had eyes that laughed
same color as them fancy shoes
laugh like silver bobbles
on a red-and-blue velvet dress
color of midnight
even in the dark I seen me
looking back from those black eyes
I wasn't scared
she shown me slow, easy
the whole field of yellow clover
bells on her shoes real soft
jingle jangle

so many nights I can't sleep
smell comes in the window after me
when my wife's alive times
I lain the whole night beside her shaking
awake, all that dark
tearing holes in me
nothing I could do but stay there
listen for the sound of silver windbells
kids in the next room, sleeping,
nobody could smell it or hear it but me
summer clover jingle jangle

he set there staring at that money
in his hand
almost like he's talking to it

like he done forgotten
I was there too
never sed no more
put it in his pocket
and closed his eyes
I could tell he's smelling the summer grass
it was all over for then

so let's take this pigfeed
out to the pens and we'll be done
lifting it down won't be as hard
as getting it in
2nd half's always easier'n first

Curley

Greater love hath no man than this,
that a man lay down his life for his friend

JOHN 15:13

Town drunk for years
was Curley Larsen
2 years Fred Lister took over
till he ruint his liver and died
Curley got it back

he's a finish carpenter
when he felt like it
until he took his drinking serious
he'd put a door in then
it wasn't no way it looked like
you could walk through
standing up straight
he'd set there drunk monkeying
till it would close and lock

got in a terrible fight
front of the postoffice oncet with Fred
when they come for mail
sed whar you going?
othern sez what you say?
sed none of your business
well I aint ascairt of you he sez
sed prove it you sonofabitch
swung on him
standing 5 foot apart
couldn't of reached each other
with a boat paddle

swinging like a tilterwhirl
Curley hit 3 times in a row
last one all the way back
went around fell on his ast
Fred dropped down on his knees
sed I had enuf
Curley sez you win I quit
Fred puked he's breathing so hard
Curley sez I'm too old to fight you
ever time you come up
I aint doing this no more
Fred sed I'm going home
my wife can get the damn mail
from now on if you're still here
both set in the street
almost a half hour
getting their breath back
neither one hit the othern oncet
so Curley got up finally
went off to find his car
whole crowd of people watching
went right by Mizrez Fortune
who was about 80 back then standing there
sed what you staring at you sonofabitch?
I don't know how Fred got home

he could save money
making his own beer at his house
in the garage and bathtub
he'd have a tasting party
didn't think it was polite
to drink by hisself
nobody else would much come
embarrassed of their reputation

so he'd go out back to the sheds
and drink with his pigs
specially this one hog
was his favorite
him and that spotted boar'd
get drunk on homemade beer
and fall down sometimes
he'd try to race him
drinking a bucket of it
but he never won

oncet drinking quart bottles
that boar'd learnt to hold it
in his mouth and tip up
like he's a man and swallow
so Curley tripped and dropt his
all spilt in the mud
he tried to get that boar's away
from him to get some of it back
before he drunk it all
you never heard such a squalling
and bellering
leggo you fat sonofabitch that's mine
I want it he hollered
that boar hung on with his teeth
squolt like you stuck him
with a icepick in the neck
Curley had to bust a board
over his head to get it away
made that hog so mad
he torn his britches leg off
trying to get it back
he'd arredy drunk over half

this one other time
he never come home that night
for supper or bed
next morning his wife was ascairt
thought he might of died
and wrecked the car
she calt the law
looked all over and put him
on the radio to see if somebody's
found him off dead
he's out back in the hog shed
where they seen him still passed out
after dinner when they
took slops out
him and that boar drunk
laying there on top of each other
car was parked in the shade
the whole time
she never looked to see

he was making beer
in a shed out back in bottles
when he got the yeast wrong
sugar started working in the daylight
bottles blown all their lids off
beer spurted out on the dirt floor
they heard him in the house
hollering like he's caught hisself
in the tractor fanbelt
come out here he yelled get out here now
come running to see
if it was any blood
go get the boar he sed
get him and turn him out

he's down on his belly
slurping beer out of a dent
in the ground
hurry up and bring him goddammit
he sed it's a draining in
we caint let it all waste

Jesse

Ugly creatures, ugly grunting creatures
MIROSLAV HOLUB

Jesse Dixon didn't have no wife or kids
it was pigpens by his trailer outside town
he raised 200 hogs at a time instead

you'd see his beat-up pickup making rounds
filling up the barrels with his pig feed
from Jim Josey's grocery store up to town

he'd get used bread and lettuce leaves he'd need
scrounging round to make up his living out there
alone with them hogs, sagebrush and ragweed

then that damn Dickie Biggins this one year
went and found the dirtroad behind his place
took them girls out to the middle of nowhere

almost half the night on every Friday
wallering in the backseat of his daddy's car
everbody thought it wasn't no way

somebody wouldn't have to marry his daughter
to him and ruin their lives from then on
anybody but him in the family cookie-jar

Jesse oncet in springtime seen him come round
when his sows was farreling babies in the sheds
watched that boy's car's backsprings bounce up and down

took it as long as he could they sed
went in his trailerhouse and got his shotgun
Dickie and that new girl was bare naked

when he jerked and slung that cardoor open
both thought they was about as good as dead
staring at the barrel end of that gun

"Haven't you got respect for nothing?" he sed
"you are a disgrace to the human race
Mothers and babies is in them pig sheds"

he's so pissed off tears was running down his face
screaming like a rooster when Dickie torn out
"Never bring your goddam filth back to my place"

Vera

The County Treasurer for years
was Vera Gollehans
who let cats live in the house
and had the cancer
back before it got popular
we all thought it was sumin different
that she got from having all them things
in the house with her

this one was old
whupped so many times
it didn't have no ears
on either side and a stump
for a tail looked like a Viennie sausage
when it wagged
and only one eye
it'd lain in her lap
all day at the courthouse
find its way home
jump up on the cupboard
squat and pee in the sinkhole
she sed it was so smart
but we thought it given her
the disease
we figgered it used the sink
cause it was too lazy to cover it up
it might not of been that one
she had about a dozen more
one night it was prowling
got in this ohgoddam catfight
all down the street
lights in every house went on

you could hear shotgun shells
being loaded from inside the carwindow
it was getting eat up good
tore out home
squalling like a banshee rooster
that other cat wasn't through
come after him

Vera's asleep
with her window open
it was August
never heard a thing
she's too sick by then
that cat come in
went down under the covers
to go to bed and sleep with her
here come the othern
they had it out in the dark
between her legs

heard her in Tennessee
neighbors come running
thought it was a tragedy
her being raped or dying
they wanted to see
Boyd Carr come through the backdoor
run in her room
turnt on the light

she's standing on her bed
with her nightgown pulled up
over her head
he sed her belly had blood
and slobber and catsnot

all over it
that cancer poked out
like she's pregnant on one side
or a watermelon grown there
her stomach looked like
whatall was in there
had a pocketknife
trying to cut its way out
she couldn't stop
hollered with her mouth
wide open as her eyes
Boyd sed it scairt him so bad
he only seen that bump on her belly
and her face
he thought the devil got her
he wanted out of there
left without turning off the light
Ellis Britton sed by god
he'd of made sure he seen
more'n that
it was principle

they called Doc Kitchens
cause it was so late
he's only one come out at night
he's drunk
sed she'd be okay soon's she sober up
taken and given her a shot
they sed Doc she don't drink
she's got the cancer
he sed it's bad I seen worst
but that's gone taste when she chews it
shot put her back to sleep

but the cat was arredy gone
we didn't see it no more

she died anyway
in the hospital a coupla months later
they just opened the doors
after her funeral
let all them cats out
then closed them up so they'd run off
and got a new County Treasurer
wouldn't nobody take one back then
we didn't want the disease

Broken Leg

John I sed how'd you do that?
It's none of your damn business
if I fell off a loading chute
and busted the little bone 2 inches
from my ankle or I'd be crippled forever
instead of just in a cast
5 goddam weeks with 3d crop
needing to be cut

you're posta ast if its anything
you can do to help out
not stand there looking to see
if its any blood showing
go get on that swoker for me
and cut Met Johnson's hay
before he passes a conniption
and has a spasm

it aint that bad anyways
back home this Landrum boy
didn't have no luck with his leg
run over it planting corn
with a tractor 9 years old
when he clumb off to see
if the seeds was stringing out right
in 3 places they sed
and put a pin still there in it
he busted it or the othern
twicet more in the school
on football and baseball
one year and the next

before he got in a car wreck
with his daddy's pickup

calt his mama that night
law sez your boy he's done hurt hisself
she sed is he dead?
law sez no but it cut his foot off almost
a big piece off the side and toes
she sed is it something he
can bring home in a jar of pickled alcohol
from the hospital?
law sez no I don't think so

I think it's somewhars in that wreck
we had to prize him loost
that part stayed in
she sed well thank the Lard for that
can he get home by hisself
or do I have to come get him
and start the car
this late at night?

he's in a leg cast up to his knee
for months on crutches
so when it got bored
he's shooting a waspnest with coaloil
up in the shed eaves
in a watergun
here they come
he forgot about that leg and foot
took off running
got halfway crost the yard
before his leg remembered
the crutches by the shed door

it all give out
his mama heard the kitchen screendoor
turnt and he crawlt in
with a spraint ankle on the good leg
and his knee out of socket on the othern dangling
wasp bites all over his face
and one up his nose swolt up
like a pineapple
she sed if it's not one goddam thing
it's a dozen
is it anything else busted?
he said no ma'am I don't think so
can you get to a chair by yourself
she sed but not in here
I'm snapping beans for supper
go in the living room or somewhere
you don't turn my stomach
so he did

he didn't bust no more
of his bones after that
for a longtime
he got the faith and learnt his lesson

so before you go cut that hay
would you look round
brang me a flyswatter or clothes hanger
unscrewed so I can get it down
in my cast
this sonofabitch has got a place
if I don't itch it I'll die
I caint get to it
I left the keys to the swoker
on the kitchentable

you can find them if you'll look
on your way out
because I sure do appreciate
your offering to help out
the sick and afflicted
as your Christian duty

The Wart

And when I passed by thee, and saw thee
polluted in thine own blood, I said unto thee
when thou wast in thy blood, Live,...

EZEKIEL 16:6

You every had any warts?
I said yes, John, I have,
in high school and then two years ago
I had a bad one on my foot.
How'd you get them off
did you have to go to the doctor?
I said the one on my foot, yes,
he had to operate and said
it was the biggest one he'd seen.
How about the othern?
John, I said, I cut one off
with a pocketknife and the other one
just went away.
By itself? he sed.
Sort of, I said and John sed
you found you a healer didn't you?

And I had to say yes because John was right
It aint never come back
has it? sed John and I said no
and it won't he said
this one I got's grown up right
between my fingers and it hurts
when I gript something
you think you can find me a healer
now when I need one?
I spoze I'll have to go to some doctor

and let him burnt it
but I'd as soon not

Mizrez Patrick back home
got one on her finger oncet
she couldn't have that she was rich
didn't want no scar where it was
so people could see she had warts
she went to old Mr. Cummings
the janitor in the grade school
for years till they had to finally retire him
then he was gateman
out to the cotton mill
everybody in town known him
wasn't nobody didn't like him
he raised us all
when we's in school
never forgot one of our names
when we got in the trouble
we'd have to go talk to Mr. Cummings
he'd make us feel so bad about it
wasn't no way we'd do that again
whatever it was
he could of cured Judast we all bet

so she went to him in the night
he taken them off
they's all gone in 2 weeks no matter
how many you had or where
she tried to offer him money
that's all she had by then
he wouldn't take it
never believed in it sez
it was a gift

it'd be ruint taking money
she sent him a card
she wrote herself and he kept it
I seen it when I's older

he was the best I known
for healing and could do it all
cured fire, thrash and warts
and could stop blood miles away
wasn't no doctor around
that could handle yellow thrash
they could do red and some black
they'd send them with yellow to somebody else
anybody to get them somewheres away
cause they didn't know what to do
but Mr. Cummings could suck it out
some of the doctors known it
would even send the kids to him

it was one baby had thrash so bad
his lips swolt almost shut
with yellow blisters and in its mouth
went down its tongue
in its throat before they brung it
he never sed a word
taken that baby
and held it down where he could
look in its mouth then
wadded up his hand in a roll
shaken that baby till it cried
its mouth come open
he put his hand over its mouth
and put his own
on the other side and sucked

he turned his head and spit
mebbe he sez some words then
I don't know
done that 3 times
give that baby back
to its mother and he sez
you clean that baby up
put some warshed clothes on it
you taken and soap and wrench yourself
before you let that baby suck
if it don't get better in 3 days
you bring it back
if that thrash gets down
in its stomach it'll die
he never lost one
I bet he cured a hundred
I never seen him do it
I heard about it

and blood he could stop anywhere
he didn't have to be there
he known the Bible verse by heart
had it welded in
he could speak it
put in the name if he known it
in the right place
blood would dry up right then
over the telephone even

not just somebody
it was a horse run into a picketfence
rammed one up in his chest
when they pulled it out
blood come out like a waterhose

that horse was gone die
and it belonged to Wesley Stevens
broke out its pen and run off
trying to find something to eat
so it wouldn't starve to death
he fed them to his pigs
when they died that way
but he'd of said they stoled it
and killed it on purpose

it was worth 4 thousand dollars
a racehorse and sued them
they had to get that blood stopped
so they called Mr. Cummings
at the school sed please come down
he sed how far is it and where
tell me what that horse looks like
they did and sez you coming?
he sed no
that blood'll be stopping about now
it was just across the street
from where they's calling
they was mad and sez he's a liar
not to his face but when
they got back that blood
was down to almost nothing then stopped
horse lived
they had to pay for feeding him
while he healed up
it wasn't Wesley Stevens' fault

nosebleeds at school
cut fingers and bit tongues
school nurse would send them

right to him
he stopped a knife-cut in a fight
that man would have bled to death
doctor sed so
his vein was cut
doctor sed it wasn't no way
it should of stopped bleeding
but he didn't believe in it
he could throw fire out
him and his cousin Grace Nelson both
she's a womern and used her breath
he called it out and made it leave
Wart Thuett we called
this one I grown up with
real name Wallace Garland Thuett
when he's in grade school
they's taking the Saturday bath
it was cold
so after they got out the tub
in the kitchen they'd dry off
by the woodstove
it was Stewart Warner
he was little then
backed up to it to get warm
backed up too far
burnt a hole on his ast
against that stove
never had no clothes on

they called Mr. Cummings right then
on the telephone
sed that boy was burnt bad
where it might cripple his leg
he sed he'd be right over

he come and looked at that burn
arredy running together
he looked down in to it sed
I'm bringing that fire up
off the bone and out of his muscle
but I'm going to leave part of it on
he'll appreciate it
one day when he's older
they sed will he be cripple?
Mr. Cummings sed no
why'd you bring me here
if you wanted that?
he pulled that fire up out of him
using the Bible words and the faith
it took about a hour or 2
they sed you could see it boil out
and then here come a word
on that boy's butt they hadn't saw
it spelled *wart* right there
where he'd backed up on the nameplate
on the stove but that was all
that was spelt on him
Mr. Cummings left that
scarred on his ast
that's how he got his name
he never even missed
a day of school and set down even
he was healed
that was a hell of a lot better
name than Wallace Garland
you ask me

Worst was when the Baker boys
not Charley Baker's idiots

some different ones
got burnt in the lye pit
during pig killing
and soap making
had this big lye pit burning
kids playing pop the whip
so they could be in the way
while the people worked
Ralph Baker was on the end
of the line so they popped him
slung him off
he went right in that lye pit
lit on his back
burnt him from his heels
up the back his head
all his hair come off

his brother Dole
2 years older'n he was
walked in that pit
picked him up and carried him out
before the wormen seen
started hollering
they run him in the house
torn the rest his clothes off
put him on a bed
that boy was hurt
nobody thought he'd live
one sez call the doctor
anothern sez do that but call
Mr. Cummings and Grace Nelson first
then the doctor after
they can pull that fire out

Grace Nelson she come right then
but they couldn't find him nowhere
she went right to work
I seen every bit of it
put her hands on top of that burn
never touched it
they had to hold Ralph down by then
took 4 of them to keep him still
she moved her hands over him
away from her like she's pushing
the fire off from him
blown on it
with her head right down
over her hands
I don't know how she stood the smell
it was bad 3 times
and when she done it
whispered the words
at first we couldn't hear
but it took all night
after awhile she whispered louder
then talked trying so hard
some say we shouldn't of heard
or she could lose the power
you can only give it to one other
I don't know but what she sed was

> There came a angel
> from the East
> bringing frost and fire.
> In frost
>   out fire.
> In the name of the Father
> the Son and the Holy Ghost

that's what she sed over and over
I didn't hear nothing else
doctor come sed my godamitey
that's a bad one
we gone have to take him
up to the capital for a specialist
she sed not yet
I aint got it out or he'll die
and the doctor sed
yas I expect he will
that's too bad a burn
for him to live without a miracle
they worked on him
never give up
it was a hour or 2 later
bedroom door flung open
Mr. Cummings stood there
nobody ever got him
by the telephone we never known
how he found out about it
face all white
his eyes bugged out like a cow's
hollers get OUT of here
goddam you you aint welcome
popped our necks
we hadn't never heard him yell
or say such a thing
except his cousin
she never jumped or missed a breath
kept on whispering and healing

he talked to that fire
like it was a man cussing it
telling it to get the hell out of here

all night that room was crowded
with people trying to watch and help
nobody left and everybody sed
it was like they was a extra one
in that room you could count
I seen it too and I was only 12
back then in the corner
I never slept a minute that night
try to count the people
in there but it'd never come out the same
always one more
he called that fire every kind
of a sonofabitch
you can imagine all night
Grace Nelson kept on working
the wormen prayed
doctor did what he could
men stood back and watched
us kids set on the floor
by the wall till the sun came up

Mr. Cummings face was as red
as hogblood
when he yelled Go
And don't never come back
he quit
him and his cousin had pulled
that fire out of that boy
doctor was as stupid as a duck
over it and couldn't believe it
they poured powder
for chapped ast from diaper rash on babies
to soak up the oil when it come up
that fire bubbled out of him

all night through that burnt skin
by morning they had it
up off his bone
where it would of killed him
it was only a burn
like you'd ironed him
with water blisters
that he could live over and not die
he did
not even scarred bad

they left him finally asleep
went in the other room
there was Dole who'd brung him
out of the fire
nobody'd remembered him
his feet was burnt black
Mr. Cummings sed oh no
why didn't somebody bring him in?
we never known they sed
is it too late?
he sed I don't know I hope not
him and Grace Nelson started over
but they couldn't get it all out
too much time had went by
it was in his bones

Dole's feet healed
but his toes wouldn't bend no more
when his feet grown after that
they grown right out
from under his toes
stuck up like peanuts
on top of his feet by summer

where he couldn't wear shoes
they finally had to cut them off
doctor sed he'd be a cripple for life
wouldn't never walk
except like a goose and limp
they took him to Mr. Cummings
he sed that's a lie
big toe was on both feet
he sed he'll walk just fine
if that's what he wants to do
it's up to him and his business
they sed would he pray over him
he sed what's the matter with you
don't you know how?
he sed they could do it
as good as him
they didn't need his help for that

it worked
both boys come through it
Ralph had to make up his school
Dole walked just fine
but couldn't jump too good
Ralph couldn't neither
so we figured that was
his daddy's fault by birth
they both driving bread trucks
to grocery stores for different companies
somewhere in Texas

that night
might of saved my life
I's burnt in a oilwell fire
where they thought I might die

spent almost 4 months
in the hospital where they sed if I didn't pass on
I'd be scarred for life
burnt all over and the rest
of the crew that was there died
except one and he killed hisself
cause of the burnt scars
all over him where
you couldn't tell who he was
in the bed I remembered
what they done that night
to them boys
practiced it on myself
called that fire all I could remember
and sed her words
blown on it and pushed it away
I lived and don't have
no bad scars that show
but that was a long time after

so when I worked at the cotton mill
when I's older
one day I give Mr. Cummings
a ride home in my car after work
he seen my hand on the steering wheel
sed how come you got them warts
all over you
don't you want them off?
I sed yas but I didn't know how
he sed when you get home
they'll be tinkling a little bit
you take and put some castoroil on
then you forget about it

I'd forgot he could do that
last year R.B. McCravey
give me a nickel and bought
3 of my warts off the other hand
he done that for Homer McCreary
where he had one on his ast
where he couldn't set down
in a bathtub and he thrown
his nickel under the rug
they went away but I spent mine
so they come back
if somebody buys your warts
keep the money so they'll stay gone

they went away like he sed
in about 2 weeks I never noticed
then they was all gone
he'd just take thanks
no money
and they never come back
where they was then
but now this one
it's in a different place
right between my fingers
and he's dead
I don't know where to go
they aint no more like him
and it's a damn shame
you caint find a healer now
when we really need them

Idyll

You could find
Charley Baker's idiot girl
in the west pasture springtime
picking dandelions
grazing with the pigs
mind empty as sky

No bother
wind rooting her curls
she was happy in the flowers
waving half-acre handfuls
of gold coins
to the cars going by

Haystacking

GENESIS 3:17–19

Put them on the bottom row
side down so the wet
won't soak up so far
we'll square up from there
goddam I'm getting tired
I hope it's some supper ready
you ready for anothern?
I'll throw it right there
youg'n snake it over
this is about the sorriest hay
I every grown
but the price is so low
I caint afford to sell it

back home oncet
my brother he grabbed this bale
to stack it and seen it move
he thrown it down and looked
it was a rattlesnake got baled
in that hay trying
to get loose
he's working for that damned Bryant Williamson
who was so onrey
my brother oncet he borrowed
the other Mexican's hat with a high crown
like they wore when they come in
he put a roll of toilet paper
on his head and put that hat on
so when Bryant Williamson

chewed his ast up that day
my brother took off his hat
unrolled some paper
and wiped off the back of his head
Bryant Williamson sed good god
and that's all
never even offered to fire him
he's too mean to change by then
so my brother real careful
slud that bale on the stack
and left it with the snake in it
must not of worked
Bryant Williamson lived 10 more years
and he's arredy a old man
snake would of probley died
if it bit him

I'm working with Heavy one day
driving tractors springplowing
a section of land
both of us
and it took a long time
we'd plow up one side
then halfway back down
meeting going the other direction
we needed a drink of water
every time so we'd stop
and go to the well
under this boardarc tree
where it was a hose
one would pump and the othern
drink and take turns
this one time
it was Henry's time to drink first

that was his real name
he picked up that hose
the end had mud plugged up
he taken and put his finger in unpushing
his eyes got big so he turned that hose up
looked
thrown it down
sez they's a snake in there
this little black racer
in there to keep cool
crawled out on the ground
that Eva McMahon had put in
back then when she's only 9
until she got back from school
and needed it
you'd of thought it was a alligator
the way Henry took off
we like to died of thirst that day
it was only about a foot
and a half long
but he never liked snakes
and got spooked

not as bad as that time
he's working at the car garage
they called him
over to Dr. Tubbs's office
to see what Wayne Runkles
brung in from the boyscout camp
where they's gone have Indin dancing
with these snakes
he's gone give some medicine
to make them drunk
do the dance with

and held some of them
in their mouths even like Indins
but this big one
they got out in the car
playing with it crawled off
through the heater
they couldn't find it no more
didn't tell him
just sed it was something underneath
he lifted that hood up
stuck his face down to see
it was a snake wrapped round
the fan pulleys sticking his black tongue out
at him about 9 inches away
he didn't know about and wasn't ready for
or he wouldn't have come anyway
hollered like a firetruck
slammed that hood on his hand
torn a fingernail off
run down the street hollering
4 blocks till he give out
he weighed 300 pounds by then
wouldn't come back to help
he sed they could haul that goddam car
to the dumpground
wouldn't even let Dr. Tubbs
fix his finger for free
he sed he'd find him anothern
to go to after that

Dan Cockrum and Hansford Hudman
put a bullsnake in a box
and when they seen Alberta Penny
coming down the street

give it to her
they told her it was some wine
but she couldn't drink it
on the premises right there
she taken it across the street
by the cotton gin
set down and opened it
hollered just oncet
for about 2 minutes long they sed
run away zigzagging
with her hands on her head
next day Dan Cockrum
tried to give her
a bottle of wine because she cleaned
his house on Thursdays
she wouldn't take it
sed you about given me a spasm
I don't want nothing from you
I'll get it myself
she stole 2 bottles
of his good whiskey
when she come to work next time
never touched the cheap bottle oncet

that summer
they had a grass fire
he was a volunteer fireman
helped put it out
and this night looking
for fires where it had arredy burnt
to water if the wind changed
he was walking in front of the firetruck
without his shoes on
because he had a blister and the fire

burnt up the stickers
like walking on carpet
till he stepped on this soft cowturd
he known it was a snake
jumped straight up
before he come down
truck drove under him
lit on the hood and mashed it in
they took the money out of his check
to fix it because it was his fault
it wasn't no snake there
only cowshit he stepped in
fire department wasn't responsible

George Bird stepped on one oncet
walking along barefooted
known exactly what it was
when his foot went down
stood there like Moses' statue
never even finished the verse
of bringing in the sheaves he's singing
that snake commenced
to whipping its body around
them rattlers scratched up
the back of his legs
it went across them so many times
it was bruises high as his knee
he never looked down
to see his heel was
right on the snake's neck
just the head out under his foot
stood there with his mouth open
sed later he could hear
that snake snapping at him

his brother Edward seen it
run back to get the shotgun at home
George never moved one inch
till he got back almost a hour later
sez I'm counting 1, 2, 3
you can either jump
or I'll blow your foot off
sed tears come down his face
but he never bawled
counted and he jumped
that gun went click
he never loaded it
didn't make no different
he'd stood on it so long it was done dead
they figured thrashing round
it broke his own neck
and choked to death on it
Edward he put it on a canestalk
took it to the lefthanded ChurchofChrist
where his daddy was a preacher studying
but George Bird he wouldn't even go
sed he'd arredy had enuf snake for oncet
he'd wait and hear about it
in the sermon on Sunday

my brother thrown one at me
with a pitchfork doing hay
when I's on the wagon
and it hit me
I thought it was a king snake
but it was a rattler
that sonofabitch thought I'd duck
and let it go on over
till I heard it rattle

I jumped right on his head
it sprained his ankle I hit so hard
neither one of us would get on
that wagon neither
we unhooked the horse and rode home
without telling nobody
what was up there until they unloaded it and then
we come back to work after that
it crawled off by itself

that's as high as I can throw
for now let's go in
have some supper and quit
I'm too hungry
and LaVerne sed she's fixing
a applepie to eat
mebbe that'll make it all worth it

so can you get that bale
squirmed up there and
finish off that corner like that yeah
for a haystack
of nogoddamgood hay
that's about perfect

Brothers

It was this boy named Phillip Chariot
his mama opened the Bible when he's borned
whatever she seen was it
they called him Bubber
he had this harelip that didn't show
inside his mouth
they all sed it must of went on up through
to the top because he wasn't very smart
it didn't matter
you couldn't understand him when he talked
it wasn't his fault
he mostly just set and nod

the other brother was real smart
went to school studying typewriter
had a good job downtown
whenever you'd ask or tell him something
he'd always say oh I know that
his name was Cephas Peter
they called him Junior or C.P.
it didn't matter
he'd say the same thing either way
he arredy knew it

Bubber one day he taken and bought this boar
at the auction
gave 2 dollars for it
it was old and not worth nothing
brung him home in the daylight
nobody paid no attention to Bubber
wallered that hog in the house
got him in the bathtub somehow

nobody seen it
got the gun down off the wall
killed that boar right there
and left him

C.P. come home from working
went in to pee like he always did
hollers and comes out
Bubber's setting on the furniture
nobody else had saw it
he sez it's a dead hog in the bathtub
they all looked around
Bubber got up he walked to the screendoor
right before he went outside
before anybody could go see the dead hog
in the bathtub
he turned around
smiling they sed big
you could see right up in that hole
in his mouth
clear as a new moon sed oh I knew that
they all heard him say it and then
he let the screendoor slam shut
when he walked out and left

The Landrum Geese

What time is it? Is it time yet for supper?
Go up to the house and tell LaVerne
to get some supper ready I'm hungry
no don't, goddam get back here right now
don't go messing with her about no supper
she's in her wrong moon turn this week
don't say nothing at all right now
she'll do it her way or not
you go and piss her off
it could mess up the rest of your life
and ruirn the whole evening
yours and my goose both would be cook

I known a man name Goose once
I grown up with Goose Landrum
that's what we called him
his daddy and granddaddy too
I never known that one
it wasn't their real names
they had Christian ones
his daddy was Harold
and I don't know his granddaddy's
but it was something
Leon or Albert like that I imagine
his was George
we never called that to him
where'd I put them longhandle pliers?

it started with his granddaddy
which had his wife and this new baby
which later would of been his daddy
out to take a ride in the wagon

with this new team of horses
he was breaking in on a Sunday
so them horses spooked up a rabbit
scairt themselves to death and took off
like a slobbering whirlwind
he thrown her the reins
grapt that baby up and jumped off
tried to holler her to keep them
headed on the road best she could
till they given out
it was too late
sed her dress blown up in her face
she couldn't of heard him if she tried
screeching too loud by then
them horses sounded like a thunderbolt farting
she'd have to figure it out
without his help
she's a schoolteacher so he wasn't worried
it's her job to get paid to think of something
he had to carry that baby
all the way home walking
we didn't have no hitchhiking back then
most people had other things to do on a Sunday

she got back that afternoon by about 4 o'clock
he was setting on the furniture rocking
when she come in the door
sed by god I'm hungry what we having for supper?
she sez whar's the baby?
he sed it's asleep in its bed
you sure are nasty you better take you
a bath after we eat something today
she never sed nothing
walked in that room to look at the baby he thought

started humming hisself a tune
got lost studying how it went
till he heard the cock
looked up and she had the rifle
pointed right at him out of the closet
he jumped and she shot
the middle rafter right out of that rocking chair
he run to the window
tried to pull it up to jump out
it was froze he heard that gun go clock
ducked down on the floor
she shot the window right on the crossbar
all 4 pieces of glass fell out
one of them didn't even break
anothern only busted in half
he crawled to the door till he heard it again
come up running hit that door
turned down the porch and saved his life
she shot that door through the heart and lungs
right where he would of been
if he'd of stood on the other side or went straight
he run as far as he could back behind the barn
where he could look through the board gaps
to see if she was coming after him
but she never
I think it's the bushing in the solenoid not rubbing
get me a screwdriver down here

he waited the rest of the day out there
by hisself to see if she'd leave
or burn the house down
nothing else happened
sed his dog wouldn't even come out
for company it was so ascairt too

stayed under the porch the whole time
he waited until after dark for something to happen
finally when it didn't
he snuck back up to see if she'd hung herself
or was hiding with that gun
got to the window she was setting
in his chair staring at the bedroom door rocking
never even looked round sed
your supper's on the table if you want it
got up and went in and shut the door
he'd never made a sound so he never known
how she supposed he was there
that one friend of yours sez
all wormen can see in the dark
I spoze they can hear through it too
it was catfish and mashed potatoes and fish gravy
with the head on looking at him
on that plate all in a bunch cold in grease
but he ate every bit of it
he didn't think it was a good idea not to

she never offered to talk about it
and he had a story made up to splain
how she got free wagon-driving lessons
that could of costed upwards of 4 dollars
never got to use it
that baby was the only one
they ever had

from then on after that
you could walk up behind him
goose him or clap your hands
he'd turn inside out with a spasm
oncet these boys blown up

this blasting cap outside Josey's grocery store
he fainted right by the meat counter
talking to Jim Kennedy about bologna and Viennies
if he seen a gun he'd go white as a Yorkshire hog
you couldn't of offered to paid him enough
to come to town on the 4th of July
they'd of had to given him a transfusion
everybody called him Goosey
from then on

that baby grown up the same way
he was Little Goose in town
him and this womern had this baby
they named George which was my friend
before she run off to Oklahoma with a Indin well digger
his daddy was a Campbellite
didn't believe in no divorce or piano music
he waited for her to come back some day
but it was too late and she didn't
what they called him then was Poor Goose
he's ruint all over town
they'd all pray for him with the sick and afflicted
even the Lard known who Poor Goose was
but she was gone for good

before that
before they dug all them dry holes on their place
before Goosey the granddaddy hung and killed hisself
after his wife took off when Poor Goose grown up
even before he got behind on the taxes
and lost part of their farm and Kay Stokes picked it up
somebody give the grandboy they called Baby George
these 2 gooses for a birthday present
to be funny about it all

but he raised them for pets around the house
so one day eating supper they seen
them 2 going off down the road through the gate
Poor Goose sed there they go
you better get them back inside the fence
and close that gate if you want to keep them
that boy run out to do it

in a minute they looked out the window
he had one goose under both his arms jumping up and down
they could hear him hollering through the wall
Leggo goose, leggo me goose
went out on the porch sed what's going on?
boy turnt round still jumping
both them long-necked gooses had leant over
and bit him on the pecker
he squoze so hard one passed out
they thought it was dead
its head down flopping like a well-bucket
and they'd have to eat it but it wasn't
othern hung on until his daddy
jerked it loose but it was a tragedy
that goose flopped its wings and give him
a bloody nose
and it broke that boy's pecker
must of busted something in there
turnt off to the east
almost like the letter L ruirnt
took him both hands to pee from then on
he never did get married by choice
sed he never had no inclinations or otherwise
it was too much pain for being married to be worth it

so after that
after all the wormen left and Goosey hung hisself
and Poor Goose and Goose Neck
which is what they called him at first cause it looked like one
was living alone out there together
for the rest of their lives
about to lose the rest of the farm during the drought
with no money coming in to nobody
before they noticed it them 2 gooses
turned in to over a hundred
you couldn't come up to their gate even
here all them gooses would run up
with their wings and tongues out
hissing and squawking like a oilwell fire
even the Jehovah Witnesses couldn't get up to their porch
they'd of busted your knees flopping their arms
then you'd slip on goose shit and fall down
they'd bite off all your private parts and ears
before you could crawl off and get away
and that saved the farm
is it a rag up there
I can wipe off this oil with?
no dammit not a clean one
one I can use on oil
you wearing a tee shirt?
take it off and give it here

M.L. Basinger come in
with the drilling and well supply
had his machinery and parts spread out
acrost his property
people started sneaking in and stealing it at night
dogs didn't help
they'd bring dead meat and feed them

walk around and take whatall they wanted
he's about to lose everything
when he heard about the Landrum geese
went out and offered them 5 dollars apiece
for as many as they'd sell him
made enough to pay the taxes
and keep the rest of the land
it stopped the stealing right now
bunch of field hands cut across Basinger's
one evening after work singing out loud
just got the gate close
there was all them geese
if they'd of kept singing it might of been all right
but they turnt round and went quiet
like something was the matter
that was what them gooses was looking for
it was like a bale of cotton busted in a hurricane
scairt them so bad they couldn't get that gate back open
tried to run but they couldn't get away
one fell down and about drowned hisself
on dry land holding his face in the dirt
so them geese wouldn't get his eyeballs and nose

tried to climb that fence with the barbwore on top
cut their hands up like it got caught in a gin grinder
tore their britches almost off going over
one got tangled up and his foot stuck
hung him head down on the fence
but them geese couldn't get to him on the other side
his face a inch away
this one goose trying to get its head through the fence
hissed till he had goosespit down the side his mouth
screamed so loud they thought it was a firetruck
all in the Spanish they couldn't understand a word of it

but them geese seemed to know what he wanted
made them so excited
you could hear it 4 miles away
had to cut him down with some pliers
they thought his ankle was busted
never found out
he hit on his head and come up running
none of them field hands said they didn't never
see him again he was gone
them geese chased him down the fence
trying to get to him heading straight south
they had them some plans worked out for him
M.L. Basinger after that put up a sign
sed KEEP OUT THIS PROPERTY IS PROTECTED
BY LANDRUM ATTACK GEESE
YOU COME THROUGH THIS GATE YOU WILL PROBLEY DIE

it was such a good idear
everbody wanted to buy some of them geese
even Charley Baker for his junkyard
and tied that sonofabitch dog up with a chain
but somebody told them idiot kids of his
they could populate with a goose
so he had to let them go
but it was worth a try he said
that dog was too mean even for him
but it never bit them idiots even oncet

that's how the Landrums got by and
held on to their land selling geese
for all them years till they give it up
but now you know something most people don't
who lived here all their lives
they think them people was call Goose

because of what they raise
that's how come nobody can pass a history test no more
they don't know before from after
and most don't give a damn either way
just what's on television and have supper ready on time
which if you push too hard on when she aint in the mood
can get you in a lot of trouble
set the whole thing going all over again
like the way it works when you don't pay attention
sometimes your goose don't get cook
you have to live with it
and that can last a real long time
get in and turn the crunk over
let's see if this sonofabitch'll start yet
we'll drive to town and buy something to eat
if you need supper that bad before it's ready

Bobby Joe

if I should die before I wake...

I don't know if I believed in ghosts
before Bobby Joe Lee had his stroke

that big man we called Bull lying there
all them years in that hospital room

wasn't nothing they could do
but wait and see

if he'd try to wake up or let it go
he was like a lightning-struck tree

didn't even know it was gone
alone in there, blind and lost

until the next firestorm come
to finish him off

Willie and the Water Pipe

Then you have done a braver thing
Than all the Worthies did

JOHN DONNE

Willie Dalton would of laughed
if he'd been there
for his own funeral
8 men carrying his box
any one could of
carried him off like a floursack
he never stood 5 foot tall
in cowboy boots or weighed
a hundred pounds a day in his life
his own family sed they thought
that doctor must of throwed out
the baby and got the other part
to breathe he's so runty

he's a horse jockey
didn't have much choice of it
broke 3-year-olds every spring
at all the ranches around
one time a man sed
in front of him it wasn't ever
no horse alive Willie Dalton
couldn't ride and he sed
that's a pile of crap
any horse could of throwed him off
on a day but he'd try
and get back on
it was some thrown him
right back off again on his ast

but he made good money at it
busted almost every bone
in his body and his privates
one time or the other

it was a 4th of July picnic
we had for the whole town
back then every year
had running and jumping
rassling in it
so Leon Bilberry this one year
whupped everybody that tried him
he sed it aint no man
in this town I caint kick his ast
them words never even hit ground
before Willie Dalton was at him
jumped right up on his head
wrapped him up with his arms
one leg around his neck and the othern
under his armpit and elbow
hollering like a strangled bobcat
he'd pry something loose Willie
would grab him another way
couldn't shake him off
Leon sed it was like a octopus
had his testicles wrapped
around his head
finally he fell down
whichever way he rolled
Willie went the othern riding him
like he's breaking a mule
kicked his sides so hard he thought
9 ribs was busted
it was only 2

till he give up Willie sed
say calf rope he did
say I give he did
say I won't never rassle Willie Dalton
never again he did
on his mother's white butt her watching
anything to get him off of him
he wouldn't rassle nobody after that

but what Willie done
that nobody else in our town
ever done before or since
was clean out the water pipe

town water come from
the mountain 7 miles
for ditch water and 4 drinking
so one spring both pipes clogt up
they fixed the drinking by geography
went halfway down and cut
it wasn't no water
so half of that back up
till they found the plug 3d cut
and got it out
but the ditch water was different
not plugged off just partly
couldn't get no full stream of pressure
they didn't know what to do
so at the town board meeting
Willie Dalton sed for 2 bottles of whiskey
I'll clean that pipe out
they shut off the water
from the dam and he clumb in
the next day crawled that pipe

7 miles downmountain
through a 16-inch hole by hisself
with a flashlight
breaking up the bumps
to the bottom with his body
all day
when they opened that headgate
it was 9 dumptruck loads of gravel
and rock come out of that pipe
he'd loosened up going through

he crawled that pipe
30 years every spring
by hisself for 2 bottles of whiskey
even after he had a cancer
like half a cantalope
hanging off his neck
his whole skin yellow as squash
almost ready to die
that last time he didn't come out
till after dark
only 4 people left waiting to see
some of the rest sed
he's dead we'll warsh him out
in the morning sometime
give him his 2 bottles of whiskey
Roy Talbert sed you gone open them
we'll have a drink?
Willie sed bullshit
that's all

they was sitting on his mantle
the day he died a month later
not even opened

with a letter they read
sed if I'm dead you can open these
and all have a drink now on me
wasn't one man in town
even Curley Larsen who would
touch one of them bottles
I expect they still setting there
and the water pipe sealt itself up
2 years later with mud and rock
they never could clean out
all the farmers had to go to wells
because Willie wasn't there no more
they had to find another way
to get by without him

Postlude

1

It's at least 2 people who'll never forget
the day old man Cummings died
I heard he's about to give it up
so I went by to see whatall I could do
like everybody else who'd known him for all their lives
it was a whole roomful of people
already there first when I come
wasn't even no open furniture nowhere
so we stood up or set on the floor waiting
while the otherns rocked or clucked

then the Reverent Jackson shown up
Reverent William Robert Jackson Lard's servant
back when we's kids growing up
we never called him that
he went to preacher school and got his churchhouse
we didn't know him no more
him and his name both got put into the revised version
he stopped being one of us for then
come in that house and sed
Has Brother Cummings expired?
I didn't have no words to answer that
but Lucille Cummings who had been his in-law
back before his boy Eugene she married died in his pigpens
face down in the mud of a heart attackt
sed Nosir Reverent but it's close
he been in his coma for 3 days now trying
the Reverent sez Brethern
let us bow togethah for a word of prayah
held up his hand so the Lard would know to listen

never got to the end of the first line
telling god who it was talking
we heard old man Cummings
call through the door to him
sed Billy Bob would you come in here for a minute?
not very loud we barely heard it
just like we was still kids in the school
and Mizrez Pennington had took one of us
down to Mr. Cummings back then
for being a disruption of influence
sed Shut the door behind you please son
we never heard no more
it felt like a little wind
went through that house shivering
looking for a place to curl up and lain down
it was after that when I heard the bells

2

he wasn't in that room but a little bit
when the door come back open
you could see right then by looking
Billy Bob Jackson had been down to Mr. Cummings
he wasn't gone be no trouble no more
for at least a long time
some sworn his face shown like Moses
coming back from the mountain
but he could of been trying not to be crying
like people have to do when them things happen
he sed Mr. Cummings he's went on now

at first he wouldn't tell us no more
I don't think he ever did tell everthing
but he finally come round sez
He was whispering soft so I couldn't hardly hear

but I known he known what he was being told
we could see that because he quit talking preacher talk
we could understand ever word in his mouth
even when he finally sed that prayer for all of us
And then it was like he looked right past me
like it was otherns in that room besides me
he stopped whispering and looked where they were
then he sez Well hello
it's sure nice of you to come
I swear that room turned warm like summertime
you'd think you could smell clover hay in there
when I looked at him again he was smiling
I could tell he done gone and left

3

they all talked about it for days and years
we should of built him a statue
but those of us who'd of thought of it wasn't expensive people
so he's just buried instead
some sed it was his wife come for him that day
some sed his boy Eugene must of been there too
the elders and deacons sed it was Jesust for sure with angels
Billy Bob never sed nothing else about it
and neither did I
there wasn't nobody for me to tell
but when I close my eyes and think about it even now
I can hear that sound I heard back then
of some silver bells jinglejangling in the wind

Benediction

Ellis Britton was standing outside the churchhouse
after the closing prayer by hisself this oncet
you couldn't be there by him and say something
you never known what he would say out loud
he'd goddam this and ohjesustchrist anothern
everbody talking to each other listening
wondering why they didn't go ahead and kick him out
he never put no money in the collection plate anyway
but they known if they did
he'd burn the churchhouse down that night
and their house too if he thought they's in on it
this one time the Campbellites across the street
hadn't quite got done and come out to stare yet
was singing the closing song right before the prayer
come to the line
        will there be any stars in my crown?
Ellis he turnt round hollered loud as he could
through their front door open cause it was summer
        no not one
        not a fucking one
wasn't nothing nobody could do
but get in their car and drive off home
one man Lovard Peacock I think back then
about torn his 5-year-old boy's shoulder out its socket
pulling him to the parking lot to get away
so nobody would think he sed it
when them ChurchofChristers come out to see
only ones left was the Brittons and the preacher
cars pulling out of there like it was Indianapolis
Ellis Britton he grapt his wife by the arm
sed let's get the hell out of here
we don't have to put up with this one bit

that preacher was so embarrassed
he had to go across the street and apologize
to all them Campbellites standing there
so they wouldn't think he was responsible
for Ellis Britton saying such a terrible thing
even if it might of been true

so this one day I'm talking about
that preacher didn't want to be polite
he walked up to Ellis Britton over off by hisself
had to find the right thing to say so Ellis
wouldn't have something to thrown a fit about
the whole congregation standing there listening to see
sed Brother Britton your wife sure is looking nice today
Ellis Britton sed oh bullshit
she's so goddam fat won't none of her clothes
fit her no more
she gets up a sweat even thinking
about walking outside to get the mail
it soaks in to the furniture
where it smells like hogs been in heat wallering on it
you caint even stand to set there
it'll slime up your clothes so bad
your britches climb up in the crack of your ast
and stick the rest of the day
you have to peel it out at night
I believe she's the 2nd fattest womern in the churchhouse
she caint find no clothes to buy in this town
even her underwears is too tight
the rubbers won't stretch enuf
and it leaves a dent all night on her belly
they don't make them big enuf that we can find
so what I want to know Reverent
is whar does your wife go to buy her drawers?

by god if they can fit her
they ought to be able to have some for my Lorene
that preacher learnt his lesson that day
after that he let Ellis Britton stand by hisself studying sidewalks
outside the churchhouse when the services was over
just like everbody else had learned how to do before he come along

Covenants

Psalm Written After Reading Cormac McCarthy and Taking a Three-Hour Climb to the Top of Pine Valley Mountain

Laughter is also a form of prayer
KIERKEGAARD

Right here, Lord,
tether me to my shadow
like a fat spavined mule
stuck sideways in tankmud
bawling for eternity

At midnight
when the stars slip their traces
and race the moon like wild horses
to their deaths in the darkness
let my hoarse song twine with the nightwind

May the bray
of today's laughter fall
like a pitchy topbranch from a tall yellow pine
straight down like winter sleet
to the mountain's bent and trembling knees

Cigarettes

Now Roy Bob Jamerson
had a heart attackt about six months
before he died or seven
Doctor told him he had to give it up
the smoking or he'd have anothern
he sed how much good will it do?
Doctor sez it'll add days or weeks
mebbe months tacked on the end
like 4th of July cotton-mill bonus

Roy Bob Jamerson sed bullshit
it aint worth it
that wasn't enough to buy
two bottles of cheap whiskey
he had this in-law
by marriage been quitting smoking
for more'n five years and he's a damn mess
with his whole life because of it
goes out to drink a drink
he'll have to have a smoke or two
when he gets home his wife
which is my wife's cousin
rattles like a chainsaw
when she smells it on him
they'll holler till he's had enough
slams the screendoor
goes to get drunk and smoke, all her fault
he'll take up with some womern
spend the whole night out
testing the back springs in his car
next day use up all his time
thinking a excuse to his wife

he'll go have a drink to help
there he goes again needing a smoke
sed it was one time
he didn't get hardly no sleep
for a month trying to quit smoking
and it was a terrible experience

I haven't got no time
to lose sleep he sed and I'm too old
to get drunk and chase wormen all night
so he told his daughter right then to go
buy him some Chesterfields or Pell Mells
make sure they given her
some matches to light them with

he smoked two or three packs of cigarettes
for the rest of his life
every day before he died
and then it wasn't a heart attackt
but the emphysema
he sed it was because
when he was a boy
he had to clean out the chickenhouse
by hisself all them years
without no help
all that new ammonia in the air
ate up the inside his lungs
ruint him
he wasn't never the same
smoking didn't have nothing to do with it

his brother said that was a fact
but it wasn't their fault
he was the oldest

got started by hisself from their daddy
he had his own way to do it all
oncet he had his mind set on a thing
whether it was chickenshit or smoking cigarettes
he'd stay with it till he finished
Roy Bob had some principles to live his life by

Whiskey

Leonard Askins was a bad one
to drink even before he went deaf
he'd work the afternoon shift
for one place and the next
then go get drunk most of the night
sed it was the only way
he could stand to put up
with working that hard all day
until he lost his hearing
he must of figured if he couldn't hear
nobody else could either
he went on Social Security
so he could be drinking full time

way back before that
he took the pledge oncet for good
had this boy in the third grade
that had a class party
for animals name Albert Askins
but he didn't have no pet to bring
they's in between dogs
cat run off or got run over
that afternoon his mama got tored
of saying no and hearing about it
some more so she finally took him
up to Wackers dime store
bought him a turtle with a black shell
out of the fish tank for fifty cents
sed now you don't talk about it again
took it home and he sed he was satisfied
made a turtle pen with a baking dish
soaked some water in it

on the kitchen table
left it there when he went to bed
next morning there was a bellering
like a hurricane bit off his ear
woke Leonard Askins up
he hadn't come in till real late drunk
and he'd told them kids
it wouldn't be no hollering in the house
on mornings when he'd been up
working hard all night
they had to let him sleep
he didn't tell them he was drunk
but they could smell the whiskey
he come out to the kitchen
sez what in the hell is going on?
I'm about to loose my patience
boy sez somebody done stoled my turtle
Daddy I name Freddy for the animal party
his mama sed it was on the table
we put it right there last night
boy sez it was on the table
somebody done stoled it
now I caint go to the party

Leonard Askins sed I don't care
about no goddam turtle
I told you not to yell in this house
when it's real people sleeping
ever one of you get out of this house right now
find you something on the way
a snake or a frog or there's dogs everwhere
you can catch you one for the day
get out of this kitchen
or I'll whup your butt till your nose bleeds

started to take his belt off
all them kids hit that door
gone without no breakfast
hollering like roosters
Leonard he could be mean
some of them didn't even have
their shoes put on
it wasn't worth the chance

he sed to his wife only thing
on that table last night
was a cold biscuit in a pie plate
with some tunafish sandwich in it
that I ate for supper
when I got home
it wasn't nothing else there
she hung her mouth open
turnt and looked out the window
never did say no more about it

three days later he was sitting
on the furniture drinking a coldbeer
when he set straight up
hollered oh my lardgod all mighty
sed you could of hammered hubcaps
on his eyes
he taken and thrown that coldbeer
right against the wall
run in to the kitchen sed
you tell them kids of yours
first one ever finds something alive
tries to bring it here again
he'll have to have another place to be
if he's not dead by then when I'm through

it won't be no more animals of no kind
here never again inside this house
took all the beer out of the frigerator
pourn it down the sink
had a bottle of Four Roses hid
that he shot with a pistol
sed he wouldn't never drink
another drop of whiskey
as long as he lived
and he meant it by god
never took a taste of it
for over two weeks

rest of his life you could almost tell
when he thought of tunafish
he wouldn't have a can of it
in his house for no reason
if he ever seen or worst smelt it
he'd retch and gag
like a dry hand pump
it was a lesson to be learnt
that boy Albert never drank whiskey oncet
turnt out to be a deacon
for the churchhouse
married a fat womern that taught Sundayschool
sed her favorite lesson
was Jesust miracles
but not the one about the water and wine
she didn't believe in that one
she loved to tell them kids
how he fed all them multitudes
made sandwiches for them
out of five little loaves of bread
and them three tunafishes

Neighbors

(and wild, wild women)
RED INGALLS

Bullards and the Bloodworths lived
down the street from each other both ways
had about nine kids more or less
nobody ever got a good count
on them Bloodworths so it could of been more
like a whole backyard full of hens
and ducks chasing grasshoppers
it was always bloody nose, skinned knee
I'm gone tell my mama she'll whup your ast
even after the sun went down
you could hear *Fibber McGee* four blocks away
everybody had it cranked up so loud
to drown them out in the whole neighborhood
especially when they ever got on the churchhouse

they'd line up acrost the street from each other
take turns hollering
    my mama sed y'all aint going to heaven when you died
    well my mama sez onliest ones there are the Babtists
    my mama sed Jesustchrist he never heard of no Babtistchurch
    well he goddam never went to no Penneycosted
      not one without no flags especially
    my mama sed them is idolarties and you're a sonofabitch
    my mama sez your mama is full of shit

then they'd thrown rocks
until one or anothern would call them
in for suppertime

one July when it was hot
Billy Joe Bullard run home
told his mama Rosemary Bloodworth
sed her mama told her
he couldn't never be no sunbeam for Jesust
Mizrez Bullard she had it
taken off her aporn
thrown it on the floor
slammed the screendoor when she left
went down the street
she's so mad you could hear
her feet in the gravels
hollered Lucille Bloodworth
out of her house
sed what did you say to that one girl
about my Billy Joe?
it was just as hot
in Lucille Bloodworth's house that day
she sed I never sed one thing
about that boy of yourn
you keep him at home
if you don't want him in my yard
is he the one has dogshit on his shoes?
Mizrez Bullard sed did you say
Christjesust never wanted my boy?
we don't have no dog
othern sez that boy never been truly warshed
in the blood of the lamb

that done it
Mizrez Bullard swung on her
like a cement mixer
next thing they both spitting
slapping and clawing

then they grabbed hair
street looked like four of Bus Pennel's hounds
slunk down it looking for a place
to lay down and die of mange in the crawl space
under somebody's back porch
hair and blood and snot all over
both of them screaming like a razorblade
just like two hogs fighting over a lace tablecloth
all them kids hollering and bellering

this one boy not theirs
was being a Indin with a bow and arrow
nine years old name Jimmy Paul James
took and licked the stopper and shot
hit Mizrez Bullard
stuckt on the bottom of her arm
where it was hanging down
she was a fleshy womern
ever time she'd give that hair a pull
arrow'd jump up and down
kids commenced to yelling like sheetiron
    Shoot her again
    Don't shoot my mama
    Let me shoot it
    Shoot her on the floppers
her shirt was tore open in the front
until this one little girl
three years old name Wanda Ann Bullard
got right in between them
looked straight up
sez mama Jimmy Paul James
done shot you with a error

them wormen let go of each other
stood right up
Lucille Bloodworth reached out
grapt that arrow and jerked it off
you could hear that rubberstopper pop
all the way down to my house
taken and broken it in half
Mizrez Bullard hollered oh my lard
I'm gone have a bruice big as a piepan
othern sez goddam ever ONE of you, who done that!
all them kids quit yelling right then
with their mouths hanging open

if he'd of just stood there
nobody would of ever known
neither one of them wormen could of told
which kids was theirs or the othern's
but Jimmy Paul James got coweyed
thrown them arrows straight up in the air
he would of strangled that bow to death
and it would of been deaf for life from the scream
if it had of been alive when he took off
for about nine steps
broke the string when he thrown
it down so hard on the road
it sounded like the whole calvary
chasing one Indin after Custard
the way they took after him
down the blocks to his house
he ran in and locked the screendoor
shut the woodendoor
went round and pulled all the windershades down
got in his bed with a pillow over his head
they banged on the door and hollered

kids chucked clods at the house for a hour
only broke one window
but it wasn't nobody home
his mama and daddy worked for a living
sed they'd call Sheriff Red Floyd by god
they'd have him arrested and thrown in jail
with the murderers and the bootleggers
they'd put one of Charley Baker's idiots
in there with him and tell it
he had candy in his pockets
none of it done any good

they waited in the sun for him to come out
and finally when he didn't
they all went home
Lucille Bloodworth sez
you keep your kids away from my chirren
Mizrez Bullard sed
I don't care if I don't never see you again
she sez that's two days before
I'll lain eyes on you
sed you go to hell you whitetrash
sez so I can hear you hollering for icewater
all the way down the street
all them kids went in the house
and it was quiet that night
for oncet

three days later
there's all them Bloodworth kids
lined up by the Bullard's car
their faces warshed and a clean shirt
Jimmy Paul James shoved in between them
to go to vacation Bible school

when Mizrez Bullard was cramming them in
one sed my mama told us
we didn't have to come back
till we had all the sandwich
and soda pop we wanted for dinner
so don't let you be in a hurry
Moses couldn't of made a dent
in them kids to see out the back winder
through the carmirror
looked like the Omaha hogtrain to Los Angeles
arms and legs hanging out the windows
wallering each other like a can of nightcrawlers
you could hear them half a mile off
singing

    Red and yellar black and white
    We love Jesust just for spite
    All the little chirren of the world

What Happened When Bobby Jack Cockrum
Tried to Bring Home a Pit Bulldog
or
What His Daddy Said to Him That Day

Son
let me tell you the story
of the man who saved
a baby grizzly bear
from a forest fire
and brought it home
nursed it
fed it
kept it like his own

And how the last thing
that man ever learned on earth
when it grown up
and he tried to keep it
out of the hogpen one morning
was the lesson
of what a grizzly bear
is at last

And it had
a final exam
he couldn't help
but pass

Rhapsody for the Good Night:
Christmas Eve

MATTHEW 8:22

1

Libations
liquid and flowing
beneath the knees of the gods

Strangest man ever was E.U. Washburn
his Bible name was Ethiopian Eunuch
come from that family opened the book
whatall was there got named
had Cephas Peter that we called C.P. or Junior
and hated because he went to school studying typewriter
come back educated where he known
the meaning of life and wrote it in a four-page paper
for the college
loved to tell about it but never got the idea
wasn't nobody listening
the other brother Phillip Chariot
we called Bubber because he had his harelip
so he watched television until Floyd Scott
got fired at Christenson's Brothers
they hired Bubber to make coffee and clean office
nurse tried to not let them name him that
but Dr. Tubbs sed go ahead
they'll call him by the letters anyway
they did so E.U. worked at the graveyard
digging and tending with Jesus Salinas

he's the baby so they raised him with Bubber
probley not talking a whole lot

when he's grown up most people or some
never known he could say nothing at all
some sed he was deaf and dumb
addled but they's wrong all three ways
he mostly didn't like to talk
he'd come to the cafe by himself
set and listen and nod

oncet it wasn't no place open to be with people
I went back to where he was in the booth
sed E.U. can I set here with you drinking coffee?
looked at me but I never set down till he nod
sed how y'all anyway? he lipped justfine
first time I heard him say anything
when we through not saying nothing
for a half hour listening to the otherns
I sed I gotta go you need a ride?
I had to drive past the graveyard to the farm
he never sed nothing then either
got up paid his bill
went out got in my truck
both of us drove to work that way
for more'n a year till I got a job
at the sawmill and had to leave early

he talk soft
couldn't play no radio to hear him
when he sed something at all

sed them's the hardest that day when I sez
it's bad about that Reuben Jimenez boy
who was in the Boy Scouts until he
died of the appendicitis when he's fourteen in high school
on the operating table without waking up

it was a month later before he sed more
that was what opened the gate
sed that boy isn't figured out he's gone yet
I dunno what to do about it
they buriet him in the wrong place
isn't nobody there to help him or tell him what to do
I sez whar?
didn't have no idea what he's talking about
he sed that Jimenez boy
longest speech he'd sed up to then
I had to think for almost a week
couldn't make it add I sez how do you know? then
without asting what? he sed
I can tell

2

nightbird
and the hum of pickup tires on hardscrabble

I listen
behind the mockingbird behind the wind
behind the sound a taproot makes
working its way down to water
past that I can hear them
theyg'n hear me too
if they want to
but they mostly don't
sometimes I talk
not to them mostly
to myself to the wind
to the field mouse under the plastic grass
in the shed by the mesquite tree
sometimes they pay attention
it's other ways too

like how they settle in to stay
or don't

Leona Huffington there
has her back to her husband
won't talk to him
but doesn't even know
he don't care

Baucis and Philemon Rojas had both
sed look for a bright spring sunrise they'd be
in bed sleeping in their morning garden
next to each other past tomorrow's dawn
Jesus thought the one plot was fine with the
headstone with one name but both in the one
red box under a blanket dressed that way
he wasn't sure of but they'd planned it through
it was what they wore their first night they wrote
so Rufus did just like they said then we
planted on both sides of their place the two
rose stalks they'd raised by their garden window
roses bloom now over the stone in a
bow bright red as Easter-morning sunshine

that other rosebush over there by Tommy Malouf
it's growing right out the palm of his hand
and in that flowerplant it's a mockingbird every day
pointing itself right at
Janie Grace Gosset who got killed
in the car wreck in high school singing
aint never a weed grown at her place
that Malouf boy give her flowers and the song
she settled right in knowing she belonged

some out there's helpless
like that Reverent Brother Strayhan
found out it aint at all
like what he been told to think
now it's too late
biggest surprises
was Ellis Britton and Kay Stokes
everbody thought Ellis he wouldn't never
fit in cause he's so mean
he was the happiest I ever seen
found out we's all wrong
he never hated the people
he hated the living
Mistah Stokes now on the other hand
he hated us all
so he aint never settled in
probley won't at least as long as Jesus is watching
can't get used to not being in charge

on a night of a full moon that comes on a payday
I seen Jesus out there with him getting drunk
telling him about all the times he come
thrown him and his family off the No Lazy S
sworn at him in front of his chirren and dog
now he sez well now Mr. Kay Stokes I believe
I'll go fishing down to the tank by the blue gate
catch me that big catfish they say down there
so what you think about that Mr. Kay Stokes dead man?

I'll swear I seen
one thousand dandelion weeds pop up
all over that grave in a night
when he's been listening to Jesus
whole grave come up three inches

he's trying so hard to get out
I rakes him back down in the morning sunshine

Ellis Britton settled
in two weeks or a month
so fast we never paid it mind
when the otherns out there saw he's ready
they started the rumor
we all have to come back do this all over again
he slunk down deep and low as he could
holding on tight
took two wheelbarrows to level him up
he just fine
a satisfied mind

3

Music is silence.
The reason we have the notes
is to emphasize the silence.

DIZZY GILLESPIE

owl say Who
preacher say whar
Rufus say here
me and Jesus
we start building
a hole in the ground
he sing
Lead me gently home Father

dying
crying
singing
preaching
praying

bringing
burying
then we all begin
the next beginning
covering
forgetting
remembering
calling
neglecting
loving
hating
moving on along

out here
back there
all the same:
wind blow
bird sing
grass grow
churchbell ring

nighttime quiet
it all sink in

4

romantic interlude
of a windy afternoon:
sunlight and elmshadow on stone

year later Christmastime
I seen E.U. of a morning sed set down
we drank coffee till the otherns left
he sed I got that Jimenez boy settled
I sez you did? he sed yas
but it almost costed me the farm

wasn't nobody hepping
they done forgot about him
all alone and scairt
down there whar it aint no time
I had to extablish a reason
they had to hep him in

I known if I could get Mistah Kay Stokes
working against my case
they'd all the rest hep that boy
I sed aint we all from the same clay?
he sed mebbe that's so boy
but it aint no jug is a vase

I sed does a man
have to come down there early
to set that boy to rest at home
cause if you aint gone do it
then I'll have to
Jesus'll clean your yard alone

that's whatall it took
Ruby Patrick sed to her own daddy
neither one's porcelain so there you go
Janie Grace Gosset sed whar's that boy?
Tommy Malouf sed I'll find him
mockingbird flown to the Rojas rose

it was a whispering in the grass
in the trees in the wind whar? sed Ellis
whar's he at whar's he at? they sed ¿dónde dónde?
mockingbird took him the song
in words he could understand
in a day the prodigal son he come home

5

in his hand a glass
filled with the moon
drowned in branchwater
or
what E.U. said
on Christmas Day

here's to the newyear
and here's to the old one
and here's to the place in between
the sunrise and the morning
between the midnight and the fullmoon
that place
between the owlcall and the mockingbird
between the roostercrow and the last henlight
under the trees under the rose
under the grass under the shadow of a footprint
that place
where all the naming and the doing
where all the listening and talking
where all the lying and the truesaying
where all the storying and the singing
where all the words theyselves
which is the first and last thing of all
slide into quiet
that dark sleeping place they can call home
just between the dreamsay
and the realsay of it all
that place
where those who know
who live there
know that without the making and remembering and telling
to help us all get on along
it aint no difference or worth finally
in none of it at all

About the Author

Since the publication of his first book of poems, *The Porcine Legacy* (1974), David Lee has written a poetry unlike any in American letters. His poems are informed by a background that is unique to the world of poetry: he has studied in the seminary for the ministry, was a boxer and is a decorated Army veteran, played semiprofessional baseball as the only white player to ever play for the Negro League Post Texas Blue Stars and was a knuckleball pitcher for the South Plains Texas League Hubbers; he has raised hogs, worked for years as a laborer in a cotton mill, earned a Ph.D. with a specialty in the poetry of John Milton, and is now the Chairman of the Department of Language and Literature at Southern Utah University.

He has published ten previous books of poetry, and is publishing a companion to this collection, *News from Down to the Cafe: New Poems*. David Lee was named Utah's first Poet Laureate, has been honored with grants from the National Endowment for the Arts and the National Endowment for the Humanities, and has received both the Mountains & Plains Booksellers Award in Poetry and the Western States Book Award in Poetry. The recipient of the Utah Governor's Award for lifetime achievement in the arts, he has also been honored as one of Utah's top twelve writers of all time by the Utah Endowment for the Humanities.

Born in Matador, Texas, he currently lives in St. George and Pine Valley, Utah, with his wife Jan and children Jon and JoDee.

The Chinese character for poetry (*shih*) combines "word" and "temple." It also serves as raison d'être for Copper Canyon Press.

Founded in 1972, Copper Canyon publishes extraordinary work – from Nobel laureates to emerging poets – and strives to maintain the highest standards of design, manufacture, marketing, and distribution. Our commitment is nurtured and sustained by the community of readers, writers, booksellers, librarians, teachers, students – everyone who shares the conviction that poetry clarifies and deepens social and spiritual awareness.

Great books depend on great presses. Publication of great poetry is especially dependent on the informed appreciation and generous patronage of readers. By becoming a Friend of Copper Canyon Press you can secure the future – and the legacy – of one of the finest independent publishers in America.

For information and catalogs

COPPER CANYON PRESS
Post Office Box 271
Port Townsend, Washington 98368
360 / 385-4925
coppercanyon@olympus.net
www.ccpress.org

CLOSING THE GATE
Colophon Farm, South 40

WE MADE A BOOK, a big, long book that took 20
years to finish and a lot of work and now it was on
the table and John and I sat looking at it, tired and
feeling good and Jan laughed and brought us a beer
and I said John this is gonna be really pretty,
they're setting the text in New Caledonia and John
sed whar's that? and I said no it's the type, a digital
version of type designed by W.A. Dwiggins for
Linotype in 1939 and John sed virgin? and I said no
he was modeling on some 19th-century Scotch faces
and John sed a Scotsman's face on the cover? and I
said no it will be that painting by Ed Cain I showed
you and John sed oh yeah that's beautimous and I
said the book titles are going to be set in Nofret, in
Misippi? sed John and I said no that's another type
designed by calligrapher Gudrun Zapf-von Hesse
for Berthold in 1987 and John sed that's purdy
young for the likes of us, you think we oughta do
this again, we ought not to quit now, should we?
And I said Valerie Brewster at Scribe Typography
designed the book and John sed I never told you
about how Arty Gill met Modean Brewster over to
Tahoka yet did I? He's my wife's grandmama
Ruby's cousin by his 2nd daddy by marriage name
Wheelis House and come to town to get teeth fitted
after they pult the last 4 riding elevators in the
Hemphill Wells store at Christmas learning to holt
them flat so they wouldn't slip and hang out on his
lips, so it got crowded and this expensive fat wom-
ern with a fycet on her arm wearing a pink collar sez

move up move up you crowding in on me when that elevator door was closing, shoved him where it caught him in a embarrassing moment like a vice grips and he was in a bind. Weg'n do that in the next one mebbe, is the paper nice? and I said oh yes they're using archival quality Glatfelter Author's Text and John sed that sounds fine so he hollered open the door open the door, ascairt that fycet where it bug-eyed, run up her arm on the fleshy part and bit him on the ear, lip and back of his head and tore a hole in his shirt collar but he never felt it, just sed please open the door, that fat womern sed now you calm right back down and let that man alone baby, lost his top plate in the doorhole when it opened and was holding the bottom one by his private lap saying oh I'm ruint oh I'm RUIRNT for life when the law who was a womern come to get him leaning against the wall for disturbing the peace holding on to hisself in public that way and he told her it hadn't been a no good time for him that whole day and I'll tell you what she sed next after McNaughton & Gunn gets this book printed and we ready for anothern about how these real-people all come together out there but right now I think we oughta drink this coldbeer and just be happy with what we got here and I believe for now we can say that's all they are to it.

for Jim & Judy Swinerton